Praise for Paperdoll

Paperdoll is a timely word for the feminine soul in our appearance-obsessed world. I'm grateful for writers, and sisters, like Natalie who are willing to bring the Word into the hardest areas of life. This book will lead you to the One who heals the most tattered of paper hearts—the One who is waiting for us at the well, Jesus.

Bethany Dillon
Sparrow recording artist

I told Natalie I was unwilling to endorse a predictable, cliché, quippy treatment of the young adult journey. I am so pleased to report that *Paperdoll* is none of those things. It is lovely, surprising, artsy and a little quirky, and every young woman should read it. It is a needed manifesto for the next generation who prefers a three-dimensional life to a paper image.

Jen Hatmaker
Author of *Ms. Understood* and *The Modern Girl's Bible Study* series

Natalie Lloyd has a captivating, personal way of sharing hopes and desires in a way that makes us realize it's okay to dream big, because God has incredible things in store for us.

Ashley Hughes
Student at the University of Mobile

Natalie Lloyd knows what it is like to live in a paper world. Through excellent exegesis of Scripture, she unpacks biblical stories and reveals their relevance to our everyday lives and shows us how to transform ordinary into extraordinary. Natalie vividly demonstrates how to develop positive self-image grounded in intimacy with our heavenly Father. This is a must-read and an essential addition to your library!

Susie Shellenberger
Editor of *Brio* magazine, published by Focus on the Family

My friend Natalie Lloyd will teach you how to live free of trying on fake identities and images in the hope that others will notice you and love you. No more paperdoll life! You can be the authentic you, the one Jesus created, the one who becomes real inside His love. Trust Natalie to lead you in this life-enriching journey.

Andrea Stephens
Brio Girl Search Coordinator, The B.A.B.E. Event

Natalie Lloyd speaks out against the image that magazines portray for young women, letting the world know in no uncertain terms that we are not meant to be one-dimensional paperdolls. It's time for the world to hear her message and affirm the beauty and uniqueness of each and every girl God has made. I wholeheartedly support any voice who speaks truth and life into young women's hearts, and Natalie is one of those voices!

Jennifer Strickland
Speaker and author of *Girl Perfect*

Natalie Lloyd

paperdoll

What Happens When an Ordinary Girl Meets an Extraordinary God

Regal

From Gospel Light
Ventura, California, U.S.A.

Published by Regal
From Gospel Light
Ventura, California, U.S.A.
www.regalbooks.com
Printed in the U.S.A.

© 2009 Natalie Lloyd. All rights reserved.
Published in association with the literary agency of WordServe Literary
Group, Ltd., 10152 S. Knoll Circle, Highlands Ranch, CO 80130.

Library of Congress Cataloging-in-Publication Data
Lloyd, Natalie.
Paperdoll : what happens when an ordinary girl meets
an extraordinary God / Natalie Lloyd.
p. cm.
Includes bibliographical references.
ISBN 978-0-8307-4784-9 (trade paper)
1. Young women—Religious life. 2. Samaritan woman
(Biblical figure) 3. Lloyd, Natalie. I. Title.
BV4551.3.L57 2009
248.8'43—dc22
008044811

1   2   3   4   5   6   7   8   9   10   /   15   14   13   12   11   10   09

Rights for publishing this book outside the U.S.A. or in non-English languages are
administered by Gospel Light Worldwide, an international not-for-profit ministry.
For additional information, please visit www.glww.org, email info@glww.org, or write
to Gospel Light Worldwide, 1957 Eastman Avenue, Ventura, CA 93003, U.S.A.

For the One who wrote grace
on my paper heart.

Contents

Foreword

The first time I met Natalie Lloyd, we were on a mission trip together in Panama. As I heard about her credentials of being a regular contributor to Focus on the Family's *Brio* Magazine and a women's devotional author, I realized we shared many passions. Eager to get to know each other better, we enjoyed several dinnertime discussions and poolside chats on that trip—about life, love, the pursuit of happiness, the pitfalls of comparison, the thrill of victory, the agony of defeat . . . and the emotional rollercoaster ride of being a woman in ministry.

On that trip, Natalie shared with me her vision for the book that you are now holding—a book to guide young women in their pursuit of abundant life, unconditional love and genuine happiness . . . a book to help them avoid comparing themselves to everyone else and beating themselves up for not measuring up . . . a book about how they can come alive in their own skin instead of wishing they could live someone else's life. "You have to write it, Natalie!" I insisted. "Don't let this dream die!" Like seeds buried deep in the soil, I knew that her idea held incredible potential to blossom into something bold and beautiful—something that would truly bless the beholder.

Fast forward a couple of years. Several personal visits and many emails later, Natalie and I were sitting across from each other at my favorite restaurant, The Potpourri House, in Tyler, Texas. While I've always thought Natalie possesses a true beauty that simply shines, she was particularly radiant that night. As we savored our spinach and strawberry salads, Natalie explained that she'd been solidifying the book idea more and more in her mind. She had decided on a great working title and had even landed a publisher. She was ready to gallop. I was ready to gallop right along with her and cheer her on.

But when she told me the passage of Scripture she was basing the book on, my mental horse came to a sudden halt. The fourth chapter of John—the story of the woman at the well. I'd read that story hundreds of times. It was even the basis of my own first two books, which had also evolved into a class I'd been teaching at Teen Mania for more than eight years. I'd preached that passage of Scripture up and down, over and over, to thousands of "women at the well," encouraging them to become "well women" instead. I pridefully assumed, *What can Natalie possibly say about the woman at the well that I haven't already said?* Not that she's forbidden to quote me or anything, but in all honesty, I was looking forward to reading the book for what I might gain out of it myself. I wanted new nuggets of wisdom and fresh revelations about how to enjoy my own life more abundantly, but I now feared that I'd be disappointed with this path she had chosen.

But guess what? I *wasn't* disappointed—in fact, far from it. As I read Natalie's wise and creatively written insights, it was like sitting across from her over dinner once again and hearing her tell a story that I'd *never* heard before. Sure, some elements were familiar, but Natalie's way of interpreting who this ordinary woman was and the life-altering encounter she had with our extraordinary God . . . well, it made my heart do triple back flips! I underlined, starred and highlighted so many passages that my pen went dry before I was finished reading the manuscript.

Having had this experience, I realize once again how rich God's Word truly is. You can literally hear the same passages of Scripture dozens of times—even teach them yourself—and yet God always has something new to teach you when you're eager to be taught. He will speak to you when you earnestly listen for His voice. He uses old, familiar words to grant new wisdom and fresh revelation.

Perhaps you may have thought, *Oh, but I know the story of the woman at the well. I don't need to read this book.* Think again. If you've ever been tempted to look at someone else—*anyone* else—

and think that your life would really be great if only you could look how they look or have what they have, this book is for you. If you have ever told yourself that life would get better once you weigh less . . . or accomplish more . . . or can buy that . . . or can do something better than anyone else can do it, this book is for you. If you've been dragging around a boatload of emotional baggage and thinking that surely your past misdeeds have disqualified you from ever being used by God, this book is for you.

If you're waiting for the good life to begin, if you live in the fantasy of what your future may hold, or if you can't imagine that there's anything spectacular about the ordinary life you're living today, get ready for a paradigm shift. Get ready for your world to be rocked. Get ready to receive not just a taste of the good life but also to have your very soul satisfied by the only One who can fill that bill. Get ready for an extraordinary encounter with our extraordinary God.

Shannon Ethridge
Author of *Every Woman's Battle* and
Every Young Woman's Battle

Beginnings

There are approximately 50 flawless faces staring back at me.

These women have no insecurities, no skin problems and no smile lines around their eyes. They all look glamorous and happy, like modern-day paperdolls. If I walk closer, every magazine cover they occupy offers a different means of securing the same self-assured happiness:

I can drop a jean size in two days.

I can take a quiz to determine whether or not he likes me.

I can learn to be a better kisser.

I can have a flatter stomach.

I can dye my hair.

I can try different makeup.

I can up my popularity status in three easy steps.

Glossy perfection isn't just dangled in front of my face when I'm here at Barnes and Noble drinking coffee across from the magazine rack. It happens when I check my email. A newsfeed beside my inbox shows me the latest red carpet walk of a beautiful actress.

Rate her, it says.

Do you like her dress? What about her hair? Is she pregnant, or did she overdo it on fast food? The picture links me to the story of another celebrity, a woman my age, who already has a condo the size of a football field and a car that doesn't rattle when it goes over 55. And, of course, she has a doting boyfriend.

All these ads, images and paper pages rush together like a whisper in my soul. They tell me something is missing. That if I have *this*, I'll feel complete. That if only I were *that* girl, then my life would be full. Suddenly, all these things meant to enhance my life *become* my life.

If you were sitting across from me drinking coffee, I would tell you what I keep telling myself: *I'm so tired of all this noise telling me the kind of woman I should become.* I'm tired of a standard that always changes. I believe beauty is so much more attainable and real than what we wear, or what we weigh, or how we look. I would tell you that I believe there is a legitimate passion I'm meant to fight for in my lifetime—a reason for my being here at this moment in history. All this fake is driving me crazy. I want real love. I want real beauty. I'm thinking you probably do, too.

My longing for something genuine brought me back to the story of the woman by a well in the fourth chapter of John. She was also looking for something real, and she was searching for it in a culture as confusing as ours. Nothing seemed out of the norm when her story began. She was just on her way to draw water. The sun rose the same way it had thousands of times before. The day was probably moving at a typical and predictable pace when she set out. The only thing different about that day was the person waiting for her when she arrived at the well. Because of their conversation, she walked away transformed, and something extraordinary happened in her heart and community. Jesus always has that effect on people. And you and I have access to that same God, just as she did. One encounter with Him changes everything.

This book has a little bit to do with the Samaritan woman, but it has more to do with how we respond to the One this book is really about—the only One who can make a paper heart come alive with passion and purpose.

You are welcome to read this book however you want, but here are some suggestions I have as you journey through:

- At the end of each chapter, you'll see a section called *Confessions*. These are personal prayers I wrote to God as I reflected on what He was teaching me through His Word. While you are welcome to pray along with me, take advantage of your moment with God and write about what He's teaching you. You might even want to buy a cheap journal to keep up with your own personal reflections.

• Try going through this book with another friend or a group of girls. In college, I teamed up with my lovely friend/roomie Roya for accountability. We were intentional about praying together, studying God's Word together, talking about what He was teaching us and holding true to the commitments we'd made. It was amazing to have someone with whom I could be completely honest about my struggles, fears and hopes. She cried with me and celebrated with me. And she lovingly (yet adamantly) told me when my heart needed an adjustment.

• Use the study guide at the end of this book, but remember that it is only a prompter. This is your book, so interact with it however you want. If you're going through this book with a small group of girls, you may want to use some of the questions during your Bible study time. Make this book yours. Write all over the margins. Underline the parts that resonate with how you feel.

• When you read about the Samaritan woman in John, or look at some of the other verses mentioned in this book, don't be afraid to tangent all over the place in your Bible. If you find an interesting study note, look it up. If you have a question, write it under the margins and ask your mentor or Bible study leader about it. The insights you pick up on your own from this journey will make it even more beautiful when you hit the last page.

I can't help but wonder what led you here. You may have picked up this book because of the title or because you know exactly what it feels like to hide behind a paper smile. You may have picked it up because you feel extremely average, and someone (or something) has convinced you that God doesn't use average girls to carry His love into the world. You may know what it feels like to be lonely and anonymous, wondering if anybody sees you as anything besides invisible. You may just think that the cover is cool. (I agree.) Or you may feel like something is missing—that something about your walk with God has come to a complete standstill. You may not know much at all about Jesus right now.

If you're asking questions about faith, love, purpose and the person of Jesus Christ, you're in good company. Those are the same kinds of questions the Samaritan woman was asking as well. No matter what the situation, I'm so excited that you are taking this journey with me. The only thing that could make it all sweeter is if we really were doing it together—if we were sitting across from each other comparing Post-it Notes and coffee stains. I wish I could hear how God will speak to your heart as you study His Word.

I think I can safely speak for girls across the world when I let you in on this secret: We have all been by the well. We have all looked for love in the wrong places and in the wrong people. But remember this: There is no place, no pit of insecurity, no hole of defeat and no ocean of sin too deep for God's love to reach. Jesus speaks life into paperdoll hearts. He is waiting to speak passion, purpose, hope and forgiveness into yours.

As I'm sitting here staring into all these beautiful faces, I can see the lipstick stain on my paper coffee cup. I can feel the fringe on my bangs (which I cut myself in a moment of weakness). I know I'm too quirky, too klutzy and too ordinary to be like the women I see on the covers of these magazines. I know that I don't measure up to that standard. And, little by little, I'm becoming okay with that. I'm slowly starting to see the girl

whom God sees when He looks at me. I've finally found something true and beautiful and worthy of all my love. I finally
found something—or Someone—wonderfully real.

See you by the well.

Natalie

1

When Paper Hearts Come Alive

There came a woman of Samaria to draw water.
JOHN 4:7, *NASB*

❀ ❀ ❀

There is One who sees my paper heart,
every frayed corner, all the rips and tears I've tried to tape
back together. Before that heart sails aimlessly through the
sky like a cheap kite, He holds out His hand, offers to keep it,
to heal it, and to make it whole again.
He writes love and grace over every seam.
Take my whole heart, *is my whisper, my plea,*
my song. Take all of me.

❀ ❀ ❀

They live in a world where people are made of paper. They are thrown together, tied with a ribbon and situated perfectly to smile at me from their clear plastic bags. Paperdolls. Blondes, brunettes and redheads with retro crops and pixie cuts.

They all smile the same smile with their head tilted in the same general manner. With just the flip of a wardrobe tab, they could be a mom, a CEO, an athlete or a hair stylist. They can walk the dog, feed a baby, or go to work or out with friends—all with that same big smile. Their hands are propped on their hips, and they wear black heels with their black swimsuits. They are part seduction, part innocent sweetness. They're '60s sitcom moms who wear pink aprons. They're peace-loving freedom fighters who wear white leather go-go boots and plaid skirts.

You can mix their outfits, though. That's the beauty of a paperdoll. They can be whatever or whoever you want them to be.

I was in a shop looking for old books when I saw them in a glass showcase. "I had a hundred of those when I was a little girl," said the dark-haired woman behind the counter. "I had all kinds of different outfits and shoes I would cut out and put on them. I guess girls like other dolls more now. Do you know anything about paperdolls?"

"Not really," was my reply. I picked up one of the bags and looked at the pretty paper girl inside. I'm not a collector or connoisseur. I only remember having a few books of paperdolls—the ones where the clothes could be cut out and the tabs folded over the doll's paper shoulders. But it wasn't nostalgia that drew me to the paperdolls in the store. (They just weren't durable enough for me. Barbies endure some wear and tear, but a paperdoll was history the first time a juice pouch turned over.) It was something else about those paper girls that caught my eye.

Maybe it was the way the sun sparkled against the plastic bags, or the way dust spun through that same beam of stray sunlight like snowflakes. I think I know better, though. Something about all those perfect paper faces made sense to me, even more sense now than when I was a little girl.

Every paper face in the box looked the same.

Every paper girl had the same smile.

Tab down the couture gown or medical uniform and she's all set. Two-dimensional perfection.

There's something about feeling two-dimensional that makes sense to me; a certain make-believe element that I still bring to the world. My doll-playing days are over, but I still tend to dwell in "maybes" and "what ifs." I still think my life begins later, in some dreamy far-off someday I imagine but never seem to find. I think God can't use me right now while I'm still waiting, wondering and becoming.

I keep trying on all these different careers. I imagine my arm looped through the arm of a certain guy. I picture my silhouette against the constant chaos of some distant city street. I visualize my name somewhere important.

At times I believe contentment will come with one of those hallmarks of young adulthood I just haven't found yet. Contentment always attaches to a "when" in my mind: *when* I have my dream job, *when* I meet the right guy, *when* I graduate, *when* I have a cute apartment, *when* I lose weight. On a good day, my heart swells in idealistic ambition. I "dwell in possibility," as Emily Dickinson would say. Other days, my heart is in more of a moody singer/songwriter mode. I wonder and worry about the outcome of a life that seems so unpredictable (a "verdictless life," as John Mayer would call it). Worry keeps me awake at night and anxious all day. I wonder how it's possible to keep pouring so much energy into people, dreams and ideas I love so much, but still feel so empty.

Paperdoll: noun

1. A paper or cardboard, usually two-dimensional, representation of the human figure, used as a child's toy.

2. Usually, paperdolls. A connected series of doll-like figures cut from folded paper.[1]

I think I know what it's like to live in a world made of paper. I know what it's like to think that if I look a specific way on the outside, everything else will fall into place on the inside. If I keep smiling, no one will see my insecurity, my fear or my frustration. If I keep my paperdoll smile, maybe they won't notice what I'm doing wrong. I think most of us find ourselves in a season like that—when we suddenly become one more pretty face in a sea of pretty faces, just another woman with a sweet smile and a torn heart. We realize too late that a smile can't disguise our emptiness for long. A distant reminder starts to echo in the caverns of our empty hearts: *We are created for more than two-dimensional living; for more than just trying to look like some other girl who has her life all together.*

I do know a thing or two about paperdolls. Sometimes, I'm afraid I'm becoming one.

Modern-day Paperdolls

I was waiting in line in the grocery store, a case of Diet Coke under one arm and a box of Captain Crunch in the other, when an interesting magazine cover caught my eye. I put down the Diet Coke with a resounding thud and started reading. The actress in the feature story was stunning. In fact, I'm certain she would look stunning even if she were standing in line at the grocery store wearing no makeup and buying Captain Crunch.

One photo showed her wearing a dark crimson dress that set off her chestnut hair and fair skin. The style experts weighed in on the look—where it succeeded, where it failed, and whether or not the slight pouf (which, for the record, I couldn't even find) around her middle was just extra fabric or a baby bump. A different picture of the same woman showed her shopping in a slightly less formal but equally hipster outfit. More "experts" weighed in on what she did right or wrong.

It would be one thing if I could always take that criticism at face value and just put it back on a shelf, change the channel or click on a different advertisement and think of something else. But sometimes I'm afraid *that* voice—the voice of a world that tells me I am never enough or need just one more thing to be happy—is one of the most influential voices in my life.

At times, whether I acknowledge it or not, those women become my standard for beauty and even my standard for living well. They become my measure for success and happiness. I get so deep in the pursuit of a name, a dream, a look, that I lose focus of the real adventure God has for me. I forget about the heart under my paper skin, the brain in my paper head. I forget there is much more to me than the girl people see.

Sometimes the art and media I fill up my mind with sends me a very simple message: *Look the part and win the life.* The look I want, the life I want, that *one* elusive thing that will fill up this feeling of empty all seem barely out of reach: a thriving career, a dreamy guy, a passport full of bright stamps. But when I look at my face beside the faces of the women in these magazines—when I compare my accomplishments to their accomplishments and measure the meaning of my life by theirs—all I see is my endless litany of faults. I even start to think that God can't use me, or won't use me, until I'm more like them.

Every paper face on the magazine shelf looks the same.

Every paper girl has the same smile. *Tab down the couture gown or her designer jeans, and a new standard emerges: two-dimensional perfection.* Perfect, on the outside at least.

Those women are all beautiful and savvy. They can all afford Marc and Stella, travel the world and fall in love. Their glossy, smiling faces are a veritable "who's who" in the high school yearbook of my twenty-something existence. I can't help but wish I could occasionally take on their lives (at least for a day—especially a day when my life is really dull), look like them, have their confidence, and know that guys can't take their eyes off me. And that's when I realize it: *I don't even know them.* I have no clue what their lives are really like. For all I know, they may look and act nothing like the woman they portray on TV, or in an ad, or on the red carpet. For all I know, they may feel like they don't quite measure up either.

My senses are flooded with the image of what my society tells me a woman *should* be, whether it's in a hair magazine, a tabloid, a fashion magazine or even in one of those cooking/decorating magazines that make me feel like a moron because I burn grilled cheese. When I'm feeling a little empty, or a little self-critical, my culture offers me a dazzling gift: wholeness wrapped in perfect teeth, a round of applause, or a weekend hookup.

In a world of glamorous excess, many people are still searching relentlessly for something to fill up the deepest ache of their lonely hearts. More cars are never enough cars. More sex is never enough sex. More compliments are never enough compliments. A perfect paper smile can only mask a torn heart for so long. There is something more to living life than stuff, status and applause. God offers something much more intense, frightening and wonderful than all that flare and glare: life abundant. He offers love that doesn't walk away or change.

My longing for something real had saturated my heart when I rolled across her story: a nameless Samaritan woman on her way to get water. I'm sure I'd heard her story plenty of times before in a Sunday School class, but it resonated differently now. Back then, I was more into stories of David chucking rocks at Goliath and stories of lions' dens that became petting zoos. The Samaritan woman's story didn't register with the girl who wanted a big, wild moment of adventure, but it registered now with the girl who wanted a deep, real, intimate encounter with the living God.

The journey the Samaritan woman made to the well is the story of one paper heart coming alive. And her story has everything to do with us.

There's Something About Samaria

If Samaria had a gossip magazine, the story you're about to read would have been on the front page. Something happened in Samaria once, something scandalous and unexpected, and it all revolves around the story of another ordinary woman with a sketchy past who came on the scene looking for love in empty places.

The first time her figure casts a shadow on the hillsides of the gospel of John, she is mostly a mystery. John doesn't mention her name. He just calls her a woman of Samaria. We'll call her "Sam" for short.

John also doesn't clue us in to a physical description of this woman. It's safe to assume that she was mostly just your average girl. She was en route to draw water—a chore matching the excitement of paying car insurance, feeding the dog, or putting gas in the car. She's from a different culture and lives in a different time, but I'm beginning to see she may have much more in common with us than I ever realized before.

For starters, she doesn't know all the churchy jargon. She doesn't resort to badly timed clichés. Her world isn't cartoony and musical; it is typical. She's more earth tone than pastel, maybe more granola than high maintenance. When we look past the surface, we see that this very ordinary girl was probably also feeling a little bit papery. The emptiness in her heart was much heavier than the empty jar in her arms, because every relationship that had promised her love had run dry in the end. She's walking to the well all alone for a reason. But we'll get there in a sec.

There is one more character we meet in the opening scene already waiting by the well. He is there on purpose. He has something important to say to *her*. What He says will change her life and transform her culture. She is going to the well empty, but the man she meets there will make her whole.

Goodbye Paper World

Most of the story of the Samaritan woman at the well told in John 4 is just a conversation between two people. As you watch this scene unfold, you're really just eavesdropping on a conversation.

There were probably pauses in that conversation, but it's pretty safe to say that the event wasn't hours and hours long. It could have happened in half an hour or less, and yet it's one of the most beautiful interactions in history. What makes this moment in time so unique is that the man who is talking is Jesus Christ—God in the flesh—and the girl talking is Sam, our ordinary Samaritan woman who is out to get water from the well. As I read her through her conversation, I notice some strong similarities between her life and mine. See if you can relate.

She Was Searching for Someone or Something to Believe in

I took an upper-level writing course in college and found my niche. For the first time in my twenty-something years, I looked forward to attending a class. I especially enjoyed being around so many other writers and listening to them read. They taught me how to make a story sizzle. One writer in particular always intrigued me. His prose was masculine and blunt, but still elegant. He had strong opinions and shared them with tact and intelligence. His thoughts on faith were particularly interesting to me. He believed that Jesus was a great man—a hero, even—but he didn't believe that Jesus was God.

This writer isn't alone. Even the word "believe" might seem like some hokey mystic catchphrase to us. I think most of us have believed in a few lost causes. We say we believe in the people we love. Many people believe there is something or someone out there, somewhere, watching over us. I've read books and listened to speakers with the message that if I believe in myself, my life will change. We all seem to be hoping for something to believe in.

The Samaritan woman was no different. She knew a little bit about religion, but she didn't know much about Jesus. At first He seemed like an ordinary man waiting by the well, but she soon realized that He was much more than that. The fact that this woman asked important questions about faith, worship and religion tells me that she'd given that part of her life a great deal of thought. The Samaritans were a religious people, and there was plenty of religion in her world. But *knowing* Jesus was different. When it clicked and she realized that Jesus was who He said He was, her life was transformed. *He* spoke truth. *He* could be trusted. *He* filled empty places. He was worthy of believing in, and He was worthy of believing.

She Was No Stranger to Heartache

Imagine having something you've done, some shred of your past, shown on a jumbo screen for the entire world to see. Imagine standing in line and seeing your worst mistake splashed on the cover of a magazine or hearing your darkest secret broadcast over an intercom. Most of us haven't had that experience (thank goodness), but sometimes our mistakes do become public knowledge. Something we did in the past starts to define who we are. Most of us come to a place in which we can't believe we did *that*, whatever that may be.

When Sam meets Jesus, she is living with a man who is not her husband. Her hometown would have been well aware of what was going on. We're also told she's had five husbands in her past. I think it's safe to say that she was no stranger to heartache. She was just as desperate as we are to be truly loved by a great guy. But romance, or the idea of it at least, wasn't filling up her emptiness. Jesus was going to use the setting of this story to help this woman see the reality of her situation and bring healing to her life. Even her deepest, darkest moment was safe with Him. She didn't even try to get her life together before she approached him. We get to come to Jesus just like that, even when we're caught in our mistakes and tangled in the past.

She Had Personal Access to Jesus

Of all the places He could have gone that day and all the people He could have talked with, Jesus had some important, specific things to say to *this* girl. The rest of her town probably didn't think she was all that spectacular, but He knew better. He could just have sent one of His disciples. He could have sent an angel. But He didn't; He went in person. He had something specific to say to her. He met her in her confusing culture, at a place symbolizing the emptiness in her life, to look her in the eye and help her sort through the chaos and find truth. I can only imagine the overwhelming feeling of belonging when she realized that God in the flesh thought she was worthy of His *time*.

When God speaks, He always has a purpose to accomplish. This is totally contradictory to the way I'm wired. I speak just because I love to talk. In fact, I often speak before I should. But throughout God's Word, whenever He audibly spoke to His people, He did so to bring about something important: a life change, a renewed passion, a specific calling, an end to slavery and oppression. When Jesus walked on earth, the words He spoke held as much meaning as His Father's in heaven. The words He spoke accomplished something in the lives of the people who heard them, and they still accomplish something in our lives today. They were recorded in the Bible for us to live by. He still speaks to us through His Word.

Hebrews 4:12 tells us that the Word of God is alive. It is as applicable to our situation now just as it was applicable to a situation 2,000 years ago. We also get to take the Bible personally. The voice that ordered galaxies also spoke to a girl by the well, and that same voice still whispers abundant life into our broken hearts. He has something to say to us.

There is something different about the Man by the well. He sees the real truth behind our smile. He knows when our smile is fake. He sees the motive behind our actions. He sees where we've been hurt in the past, and He wants to make us whole again. And He wants all of us—the brave part and the insecure, the bright and brooding. We get to bring the mess of who we are to Him and sort it out there in His presence. Just like the story of the woman at the well in John, He offers us His time. Sam found Him waiting by the well. He's waiting to move in our lives and in our culture as well.

She Took Advantage of Her Time Alone with God

For me, the most iconic image of my culture comes from a summer I spent in London. On many rainy days, I found myself surrounded by the chaos of Piccadilly Circus. It was loud, and crowded, and chaotic, and fabulous. There were bright lights, stores, advertisements, traffic, people and theater all meshed together in one place, like a moving abstract painting. That part of London was so busy and loud that I could hardly hear anything. I had to focus on what my friends were saying. I had to focus on one sign to read. The place was such an extreme sensory overload that I could barely hear myself think.

Media saturation has a way of creating this veritable Piccadilly Circus in my brain. My culture tells me the kind of woman I should become in hundreds of different mediums, languages and packages. I see the ideal woman online, on billboards, on TV, in movies and on magazine covers. In the end, it all just feels like noise. I'm tired of measuring my worth by a cultural standard that always changes and contradicts itself. God's unchanging Word is the only real source for figuring out who I am and the woman I'm becoming—a calling much more authentic and beautiful than airbrushed paper.

That's why I've got to get away from the noise and be alone with Him. He has something to say to me one on one. His Word is more than just history and instruction; it fans open like a love letter, encouraging me, giving me hope and reminding me that I have his full attention. Prayer, even in all its strange mystery, feels so intimate when I take time to do it. I know He hears every word, even when I'm too tired or frustrated to actually speak.

Society screams. But in His Word, God says He comes as a gentle whisper (see 1 Kings 19:12). Author Margaret Feinberg says that God whispers so we'll get close enough to hear what He is saying.[2] When God whispers purpose and victory over our hearts, He completely drowns out the screams of a fake paper world.

You don't have to put your name on a waiting list to talk to God. You don't have to fire off a holy text message and hope for a speedy answer. Just like He was waiting for the Samaritan woman by the well, He is waiting and ready to hear what's on your mind. Open up the communication line in your heart to God on a constant basis. Be authentic in your prayer life, just like the woman at the well was authentic when she spoke with Jesus. The girl He created is the girl He loves, so you get to be you.

There were really two empty vessels by the well in Samaria that day. One was the jar in the Samaritan woman's arms, but one was the Samaritan woman. All she really brought to the well that day was herself and a willingness to ask questions and be filled up. Start there. Let God speak to you through His Word. Get lost in the candid mystery of prayer. Get to know the Man by the well.

She Realized God Was Active in Her Everyday Life

When Bryce asked me to be her "show and tell" for class, I couldn't turn down the invite. I was too intrigued. I imagined standing in front of her classroom beside hamsters running on wheels, which thankfully wasn't the situation (the hamsters would have been far more entertaining). I ended up spending the whole hour with a fun group of seventh graders, talking about writing. Several students stayed after class to show me something they'd written. Their notebooks and folders were full of snappy prose and elegant poetry inspired by everything from shooting free throws to babysitting. *That* is why I love spending time with artists. They see beauty in the world where other people don't always see it. They have a knack for finding something extraordinary in an ordinary moment.

While I'm learning to become more intentional about spending time alone with God, I also want to learn to be more aware of His constant presence in my life. He never leaves, and Romans 8:28 tells me He's working in all things for my good. Ever the artist, God is at work in every circumstance, turning up beauty even when I see nothing beautiful.

The Samaritan woman spoke with Jesus face to face on an ordinary day while she was doing a chore. I wonder how my ordinary would be different if I thought about Him standing beside me. How would Jesus react in this argument I'm having? What would His arms feel like wrapped around my shoulders right now while I'm crying? And what if God has something to teach me right here in the middle of my boring ordinary life that changes the way I see everything?

"Get into the habit of saying, 'Speak Lord'," writes Oswald Chambers, "and life will become like a romance."[3] Endings suddenly wrap into new beginnings. Ministry happens in places we never thought possible. We're suddenly surprised by familiar details like hard laughter, new ideas and starry skies. Anybody can find beauty when it's obvious. Finding subtle beauty and looking for a holy moment in an ordinary day is more of a challenge. And it is usually far more amazing.

She Learned to Root Her Worth in One Perfect Love

The amount of effort and energy we put into finding love seems like a relentless scavenger hunt. We leave no corner unturned. We search through our school, our circle of friends, our jobs, anywhere to find a love that will give us meaning.

I can think of some stupid things I've done hoping for one nod of approval. I've looked for perfect love in the wrong places. I've given too much of my heart to something (or someone) that never loved me back and made my heart seem like a giant jigsaw puzzle with a missing piece. Even when a fleeting imitation of love numbs the emptiness, the feeling is still there.

That day by the well, Sam was reminded there is only one perfect love. Just One. It had never been hiding from her. Love at its most real and beautiful had been waiting all along with open arms to bring her the kind of acceptance that truly filled her heart to overflowing. It is through this same perfect love of God that we can love better and be loved more fully. Apart from His love, we're on a scavenger hunt with no point in sight.

The only thing that changed about the Samaritan woman's day in John 4 was meeting Jesus. One encounter with real love transformed her life.

The story of the Samaritan woman clued me into the fact that the happily ever after I keep dreaming about isn't in some

distant someday. God has a work for me to do right now. I sometimes forget that He is mine, daily. I am not loved when I become that more brilliant, more beautiful, less klutzy version of
me. I am loved now. Infinitely and completely. I don't want to
miss that.

Him and Me

One of my favorite songs is "You and Me" by the band Life-
house. The song is all about a guy who is so taken with a girl
that it's like no one else is in the room—like time itself is standing still. The more I read the story of the woman by the well, the
more it reminds me of a love song. Jesus was waiting for her,
just her, at a moment when she was searching for real love and
questioning what really mattered. When we feel as if we are fading and blending into a row of perfect paper, He comes looking
for us as well. He initiates a conversation with us. He sees the
girl we aren't brave enough to see yet; the girl who is already
beautiful, who has an incredible purpose.

You are not average or ordinary or created for designer con-
formity. An ordinary girl whose heart reflects the unconditional,
radiant, all-consuming extraordinary love of God is extraordinary. *His love makes you extraordinary.*

You were placed at this moment in history for a reason.
Your birth was no surprise to God (even if it completely took
your parents by surprise). He planned it and anticipated it, because there's a place for you here. You have a set of talents and
gifts that are unfolding inside of you. You have a personal invitation to spend time with Him whenever you want. All it
takes is one girl who will be obedient to the calling that God
places on her heart to change the world. Adventure starts here
in the ordinary.

I don't think it's a coincidence that I keep finding myself
drawn to the woman at the well at this point in my life. I am
desperate for something real. I am desperate for a love that will

not walk away. I am aching to peel off the fake paper shell and be the girl God created me to be. I needed to see what the Samaritan woman saw: the person of Jesus Christ waiting for me right beside my deepest well, my darkest point of obsession, my fear and heartbreak, offering me life abundant.

I've been just another starry-eyed paperdoll. I've been the girl who puts on whatever someone else tells me I should put on. I've tried to become whatever others wanted me to be. I've wasted so much time wishing I were some other girl or wishing my life were like somebody else's life. I've ached for acceptance. I've drowned in jealousy. I've worn the label and listened to the right bands, liked the right art, taken up a better pastime all trying to be someone—*anyone*—who mattered. When I do this, I lose my anchor. Like a tattered kite, I sail somewhere new when the wind blows. When there's fire, I am always ashes; but when it rains, before I shrivel into nothing, the last thing I see is what's written on my heart in permanent ink—a mysterious invitation to be beautiful and be real.

When I'm close to Him, my origami heart starts to beat and dance again. I finally start to come alive.

Confessions

Lord, I can think of so many ways I've tried to fill up the missing pieces of my heart with something other than You. Thank You for Your Word and for the power it has to change my life; make me think and stir my imagination. Thank You for letting me see the unfolding story of the woman You met at the well. As I become more intentional about spending time alone with You, I pray that You'll help me to keep this commitment. I know You have me here at this moment in history for a special reason. I don't want to miss it. And I don't want to miss any moment I have a chance to know You more.

Notes

1. Dictionary.com Unabridged (v 1.1), Random House, Inc., June 22, 2008, s.v. "paper doll." http://dictionary.reference.com/browse/paper doll.
2. Margaret Feinberg, *God Whispers* (Orlando, FL: Relevant Books; 2002).
3. Oswald Chambers, *My Utmost for His Highest: Updated Edition* (Grand Rapids, MI: Discovery House Publishers, 1992), January 30.

2

Love Like Water and Chaos

*Now he had to go through Samaria. So he came to
a town in Samaria called Sychar, near the plot of ground
Jacob had given to his son Joseph. Jacob's well was there,
and Jesus, tired as he was from the journey, sat down
by the well. It was about the sixth hour.*

JOHN 4:4-6

❋ ❋ ❋

*I want love that is infinite, not flimsy. I want to experience
the kind of love that boggles my mind with its depth
and dimension. I want a love I can hold up to my heart like a
kaleidoscope. Change the way I see things. Change the way I live.
Teach me how to love. Take this beautiful mess and make
it a masterpiece. Love won't shatter my heart with conditions.
It accepts, uplifts, and redefines.
I want a love that gives me peace; a love that wraps around
my shoulders like a blanket, pulling me close, whispering, "welcome home."
I want a love like chaos, stirring my imagination, igniting me with
passion, showing up in places I never expected.
I want a love I can swim in. I want to dive deeper and deeper and
move faster against the current until I feel as if my lungs are going to
explode. And then, when I break the surface, I want love to be my
first furious breath of air—intoxicating, invigorating, alive.*

❋ ❋ ❋

I live in a city snuggled deep into a line of beautiful mountains.
It's southern and quirky; a little bit traditional, a little bit trendy.
Every time I walk downtown, I remember why it stole my heart

in the first place. Dance steps are imbedded into the sidewalks, bridges thread back and forth across the water, and artists sell their paintings on street corners. There is also the appropriate theater showing a decent mix of box office hits and random indie films. Ever so often, the theater even does a cheap showing of a classic '80s movie, with all the big hair and the synthesizer-driven soundtracks, all on a big screen. It is fabulous.

My brother, Chase, and I drove there recently to watch a showing of *Back to the Future*. Toward the end of the movie, Marty McFly comes to a critical impasse. He gets back from the past early and sees *himself* standing across the parking lot in the same acid-washed jeans and puffy vest he left wearing. This is bad news. If he accidentally sees himself, he might implode (or something like that). So he ducks down behind some bushes and waits until the old Marty blasts into the past. Then the new Marty runs down the hill to save his friend.

Maybe it was me being a little confused, or maybe it was the stale popcorn, but I started thinking of how bizarre it would be to go back in time and see myself at some other point in my life. If I could choose, I think I would get in my clunky time machine and go back and visit the college me. I was incredibly shy then, and I usually felt a little bit lonely. I also became supremely confused about what love really meant and looked like in a life. It would be nice to zip back in time and spare that girl some heartbreak. So, if I could fire up the flux capacitor, go back to college and give myself some advice (which would be weird, but work with me here), I think there are three things in particular I would say. The first piece of advice would go something like this:

> *Soon you will see a movie with Ashley Judd, and you will think her haircut is cute. You'll make one of your notorious snap decisions to go get yours cut the same way, except it will not look cute on you. You won't look anything like Ashley Judd. You'll look more like Peter Pan's ugly step-sister. Don't do it.*

After I cleared that up, I would settle in for a more serious talk. The second piece of advice might be:

You are finally starting to dip your toes into a culture with many pristine imitations of love. And those imitations are starting to get to you. You're actually starting to believe that being loved is the same as trying on a new identity. But when one identity doesn't work, you tab on another one like some co-ed paperdoll. You keep letting things and people define you. You're disconnecting from the love that you know is real and true.

Don't misunderstand me. It's okay that you're trying to get something from this experience. Go see the world. Read brilliant books that make you laugh and cry. Go to concerts with your friends and sing along loudly. Make new friends. Fight losing battles. Live this moment completely. You're going to be so glad you did all that. But it will mean more if you do it out of the overflow of God's perfect love.

Your Bible is becoming another textbook. Worship is becoming a Sunday requirement. And you are becoming bizarrely obsessed with what people think of you. Your worth isn't tied up in what others think about you or whether or not they know your name. You're wasting too much time trying to figure out ways for people to love you. In the end, it's just going to make you feel more alone. Love isn't some stupid accessory or achievement you can strap onto your arms. It is deeper than that, and you know it. So stop acting like a paperdoll.

I wonder if I would have listened to advice like that. I mostly felt like I was spinning in circles during those four years in college. I changed my major many times. I studied in London, dyed my hair and read weird poetry. I joined a random assortment of campus organizations. I tried Greek life, but it wasn't a good fit. I tried a new campus ministry. That wasn't a good fit either. I went to huge churches with full bands and big screens. I went to small churches where people actually remembered my name. I volunteered in the community. I tried waxing my eyebrows (big improvement) and cut my hair short and fringy (bad idea).

None of that in and of itself is a big deal. But four years after I packed up my Civic to go to school, I packed it up again, feeling exhausted and defeated. Ever so slowly, I'd become another paperdoll, thinking that if I changed the exterior I would finally feel whole. I thought that eventually a confident creature would bloom out of the shy, artsy wallflower, but the harder I tried to belong, the more lonely I felt. If you passed me on the sidewalk in college, you would have noticed I smiled a lot. But my smile was more of an involuntary reflex. On the inside, I was crumbling.

The last piece of advice I would give the girl who wrote poems in her dorm room—who was a little bit enamored by sunsets and sonnets and the way the stars sparkle over the mountains—would be something like this:

> *You are not alone in this, so stop disconnecting yourself from the love that tore through heaven and earth to find you. Look people in the eye when you talk to them. Move into your life with courage, not fear. Start living like a girl who is loved. Don't waste any more time. Walk away from this well, paperdoll. There's a big life out there for you to live.*

If we could sit down and interview the Samaritan woman and ask her what advice she had for girls 2,000 years after her journey to the well, I wonder if she would encourage us to do something similar. We're still looking for love in all the wrong places, just like she was. We're still coming up broken, just like she did. I'm sick of twisted love and imitation fullness. I am desperate for something real, and so was she. There are many loves we get to experience in this lifetime and many adventures, people, and opportunities that will add to the beauty. But there is only one perfect love.

Looking for Love in the Wrong Places

Even though we aren't overwhelmed with details about Sam's history, John gives us some insight up front into one well-known fact about our girl in Samaria: she probably didn't fit in, either. In fact, based on what we know about her culture and her current situation, Sam may have been shunned by the people in her village.

Early on in this passage, John provides some crucial clues to her social status. First, he tells us that she was walking to the well alone (see John 4:7). Second, he mentions *the specific time* she was moving toward the well: "Jacob's well was there, and Jesus, tired as he was from the journey, sat down by the well. It was about the sixth hour" (v. 6). Most scholars believe the sixth hour would have been around noon. It's the hottest part of the day on a dry piece of land, and she's walking solo. As you picture the scene in your mind, it's important to keep those two facts at the forefront.

There are plenty of details that John didn't feel the need to mention. We aren't given any specifics about her physical appearance. We can only imagine the details of her face and personality. We don't know her age. We don't know if she walked in silence or sang a song or started humming or just walked, lost in thought. I wonder if she was holding on tight to her water jar. I wonder if her shadow stretched out like a long black veil on the hill behind her when she walked.

We have to imagine the finer details of the setting as well. The way the fields might have looked snuggled into the high hillsides, blooming and harvest-ready. The way the high rocky slopes of Mount Gerizim cut a jagged line across the Judean horizon. Yet even though we do not get a specific picture of the Samaritan woman's physical appearance or her surroundings, we do get insight into the condition of her paper heart. And her heart, at this point in her life, was frayed.

Somehow, I don't think this girl was a prom queen.

One thing in particular that is missing from this trip to the well is a group of other women. Throughout the Bible, we see examples of women together (see, for instance, Genesis 24:10-12.) The way we women travel *en masse* seems to be a cultural caveat; one of those involuntary urges that somehow baffle the men in our lives. Like how we always reach for the person beside us when we slam on the brakes (even though they're already restrained), or how we never pull up close enough to the ATM machine to get cash without actually opening the door, or how we have some sudden OCD urge to straighten a collar or grab a stray hair. And whether we're going to the mall or to the bathroom, we tend to travel in a herd. Many women tend to measure friendship in physical proximity. Whether you have one best girlfriend or a group of them, spending time with them seems to make any day a little bit brighter.

It's doubtful that Sam had that kind of relationship with the women in her village. Not only is she walking to the well alone, but she's also walking during the hottest part of the day. That move still keeps scholars arguing over coffee. Why would she wait until then to go get water? Was that just a fluke decision? Was that just when the water ran out? Or was there another reason? Was she not welcome to even tag along when the other women went to the well? Was she trying to avoid all the gossip and sideways glances? Girls who pretend to be your friend one minute can become catty, immature and cruel in the next. I doubt the passage of time has changed things.

We don't know exactly why she headed out alone, but we do know that she wasn't Samaria's "it" girl. Her reputation was a little bit shady. She probably didn't get much love from her peer group. And the rejection factor didn't stop when it came to how the other women treated her. Eventually, we will see one particular area she went looking for love that was leaving her empty.

We all have days that feel as lonely as Sam's walk to the well. Most women can vividly remember their most acute moment of feeling deserted, whether that moment lasted five minutes or five years. Maybe it was the day we sat alone in our dorm room, feeling shy, afraid and insignificant. Maybe it was the day we sat alone (again) in the cafeteria, or the day everybody seemed eager to point out the mistakes we'd made. Maybe it was the day we tried to put on a paper smile to numb the cold truth freezing our hearts: that something was still missing and no matter what we tried, we couldn't figure out what it was.

Age and circumstance don't lessen the sting of loneliness. I think we have more in common with Sam than we realized. Somewhere along the journey, we wonder if there is more to life than all the paper. We wonder if there is more than just the girl people see. Even on ordinary days we dare to believe there is something more we are made to do, experience and be in this life than just a paperdoll.

For the Samaritan woman, the paper life was about to end. The well was about to become a symbol for all the places she'd gone (unsuccessfully) looking for perfect love. And the man waiting there is going to offer her a deep, beautiful life that she probably didn't even feel she deserved. She had looked for love in some empty places, but that day love was waiting to show her what she'd been missing.

The more I picture Sam's journey there, the more I start to ask myself a rather uncomfortable question: *Where am I trying to find the love that only God can truly give me?*

There is no love that will satisfy our deepest thirst like His. The kind of love, and life, Jesus offers isn't just a textbook-no-frills-hard-faced religion. He offers a love that we can know and feel, a love we can taste and see, a love that is permanent. He offers a love that rips the paper mask to shreds.

Modern-day Wells

Even though we're just eavesdropping on this scene in Samaria, Jacob's Well is about to become an important symbol for us, too. Take a look at this verse that Jeremiah, the prophet, spoke to his people:

> For my people have done two evil things: They have forsaken me—the fountain of living water. And they have dug for themselves cracked cisterns that can hold no water at all (2:13, *NLT*).

Even though Jeremiah was talking about the Israelites, this verse can also describe a paperdoll heart. Wells are not a thing of the past. Two thousand years removed and half a world away, we have a well, too. Ours isn't made of stone and funneled deep into the craggy ground like Jacob's Well. In our lives and culture, a "well" represents anywhere we go looking for perfect love besides the love of God. A well is what we depend on to get enough of a burst of belonging and acceptance to carry us through the day. A well makes us feel validated for a little while but never really satisfies the deepest longing of our hearts. We keep going back to it for more and more until we feel consumed by it.

I know God created me to experience many kinds of love in my lifetime. I think He likes to see me enjoying the world that He created for me and living life fully. He's stirred up intense longings in my heart for romance, for a career that matters, for a cause to fight for, for a family I love and for solid friendships. But even those things can leave me feeling drained if I'm depending on them to make me whole.

There are many wells I run to for imitation love, but there are a few in particular that have a way of grabbing my attention.

Wells of Discontent

Occasionally, I have the kind of day in which I decide I need a random assortment of stuff to make my life more complete. Every article of clothing I own is on my bed or on my floor, because nothing I have looks good on me. I spend money on more

clothes I don't even need or really even want. The same princi-
ple applies to the life I'm living: no career I envision makes me
happy. I let my mind spiral into what I do not have, while I
compare my life to some other girl's. The inevitable flip-out
that follows becomes a worry residue I can't scrape off.

My culture has a keen obsession with stuff as well. Billboards splayed with gorgeous ads line the streets. Women (and
men) make retail therapy a veritable sport. Yet owning more
things—even the newest and best and trendiest things—never
brings the peace I think it will. It only makes me want more.
None of these things can buy love, and without love, I'm spent.
A little flicker of world consciousness usually helps the real me
resurface. I flip through pictures from a mission trip and see
kids happily playing with sticks and coke bottles and realize
that something is off balance in my heart.

Wells of Popularity, Status and Approval

Most of us hope that once we leave high school, we'll also leave
behind the ridiculous amount of drama that high school en-
tails. Sometimes we do, but an obsession to fit in can morph
into a lifelong monster if we allow it. There is always some version of the popular table in the high school cafeteria. You
could be 60 years old and still thinking that if only you could
just sit *there,* your life will be so enhanced. Even now, I occasionally have to back up and ask myself some important questions: *How far will I go to win the approval of other people? Am I
willing to sacrifice my integrity if it means gaining some notoriety?*
I know I'm living in a danger zone when someone's opinion of
me becomes more important in my mind, my life and my actions than God's opinion of me.

Here's the not-so-glittery truth about sacrificing morals in
the name of acceptance: Whatever you and I have to do to *make*
friends is what we will have to do to *keep* those friends. Popularity isn't always a notorious state of being. Sometimes it's also
a direct result of genuine kindness. But popularity will never

be the same as real love. The Samaritan woman's social status wasn't noteworthy. But that didn't matter to God. Her social rank didn't affect how He would use her to change history.

Our worth isn't wrapped in what other people say about us, either. Our worth is woven into the fabric of God's Word, into the ultimate truth that sets us free to be the unique, beautiful, godly women we were created to be. Pageant queens, trombone players, theater girls, bookworms, geeks and glamour girls can all take heart. It doesn't matter where we rank in life's silly social hierarchy. We've never been unnoticed by God, and He has a message for us to carry as well.

Wells of Self-absorption

I subscribe to a fashion magazine that leans heavily on the conceptual (the clothes would look fairly ridiculous on 99.9 percent of the population). It's ironic that I even like reading it, because I'm not a trendsetter. It's just that sometimes the layouts look like art displays. I like the color and chaos, and I like reading about what inspired a designer to create a line or what made him or her want to put certain textures and patterns together. I think fashion can be a cool representation of a person's individuality. But I know that beauty isn't just in a textile, a layout or in a confident runway stomp. Beauty is just as readily—and often more clearly—seen in the aisle of a grocery store or in the corner of a library.

I'm conscious of my self-image. I put thought into what I wear. But in a culture that has a tendency to define beauty in a jean size or body type, I have to keep reminding myself that there are many different kinds of beautiful. When my face and body become an obsession, I start to sink into emptiness again. It doesn't matter whether I'm obsessing over something good or, more typically, something I don't like about myself. Obsessing generally just leads to more obsessing.

In his book *The Bible Jesus Read*, Phillip Yancey shares this example of self-awareness gone awry: "Carl Jung [the well-known psychologist] reported that a third of his cases suffered from no definable neurosis than 'the senselessness and emptiness of their lives.' He went on to name meaninglessness the general neurosis of the modern era."[1]

I'm trying to live in moderation; trying to take care of the body God created and see myself in a positive light without getting dangerously obsessed. I never want to spend more time thinking about myself, even what I dislike about myself, than I spend thinking about things that matter. I'm convinced most of that obsessing just comes from wanting to be loved. I think that ideally, each of us wants to be accepted, even with all our fabulous quirks. But I would guess most of us have tried to change something in the hopes that we'll be loved more when we do.

There is much more to you than what people see (and you are probably way more beautiful than you realize). Love has a way of redefining beauty.

Wells of Obsessions and Addictions

Addictions and obsessions are such clever disguises for perfect love because they give us a temporary sense of total control. When that brief moment passes, the emptiness is overwhelming. What looked like total control turns out to be only total dependency on something that leaves us feeling defeated. We convince ourselves we will never take another pill, never take another drink, and never purposely put another scar on our bodies. Emptiness washes over us in a numbing wave of guilt when we feel the grainy tile on the bathroom floor under our fingernails, and we swear that is seriously the last time we will ever throw up on purpose. Those addictions and obsessions quickly spiral into something deadly, but there are others that have a way of subtly infringing on living a full life in a way that consumes days, hours and months of our time and makes us feel enslaved and alone.

That's the thing about Sam's story: Jesus was there even in her loneliest moment. We are never alone in our addictions and obsessions. We never have to sit in a church pew with a paper smile and pretend we don't have struggles. Jesus didn't stop by the well (or die on a cross) to point out our weakness and shame. He died to save us. He died, and He lives, to give us freedom. Jesus could have pointed out Sam's place of pain in front of her whole village, but He didn't. Ridicule was the way of the Pharisees; Jesus was all about grace.

Psalm 86:15 tells us that God is slow to anger, abounding in mercy and love. He is for us, not against us. He pulls us back up, away from the well of addiction and the emptiness, so you can walk in victory, not defeat. God doesn't save us to make an example of us; He saves us because He loves us.

Choosing to live a genuine life in Christ doesn't mean that we become perfect and suddenly incapable of making bad decisions. It means that when we do fall, we hold onto Him tightly, we get the help we need, and then we get back up. We fall and get back up. We fall and get back up.

No matter how hard you've fallen, you get to stand up, surrounded by His marvelous grace.

Wells of Romance

Over the course of my short life, I've observed guys in many different situations and contexts. Many things about these creatures intrigue me. I wonder how they can eat their weight in pizza and not gain a pound. I wonder how they make a burp sound like it actually has some sort of musical intonation.

But one question rises from all the rest: How can they always be *that* handsome? How do they drive for hours with the windows down and still look tough and rugged instead of skanky and windblown? How do they play sports for three hours—*three hours*—and still look gorgeous? And why is it that when some guys talk to me or smile at me, I feel as if my heart were going to explode? I thought the butterflies would finally subside once I got a little bit older, but I was wrong. One of my girlfriends can compliment me on the shirt I'm wearing and I'll say "thanks" and usually not remember it an hour later, but when a guy says it, I remember the compliment every time I pull that shirt out of my closet.

Just being close to them makes us feel special. Few things can seem as comforting as a guy wrapping his strong arm around us and letting us cry against his shoulder. There is something so sweet, so good and so right about romance. But if it occurs outside of God's leadership and apart from His timing, our hearts will be poised to shatter.

Falling in love seems so simple in the movies we watch and the novels we read, but so complicated and unstable in real life. In reality, we have to learn to hold our head high through rejection. Sometimes, we have to survive years of being picked over and pushed aside. I've already seen how romance, even when it starts at its best, can leave me feeling like pond scum. Suddenly, my heart is in a perpetual state of broken, just this goofy looking duct-taped mess because I was sure—positive, in fact—that when I threw it out to that guy he would keep it safe and make me feel complete.

We live in a culture with a skewed perspective on love. We treat it like a trend and forget about the weight of responsibility and commitment in those four letters. Depending on where you grew up or what's gone on in your past, the word "love" may not even mean anything to you anymore.

I believe romance, when it is real, is exceptionally beautiful. But it can also be one of the deepest and loneliest wells we can ever dig for water. The Samaritan woman knew all about that kind of heartache. At some point in her life, she'd lost five men who mattered to her. And now, when we meet her, she's living with a man she's not married to, giving away even more of her heart with no guarantee or commitment of his love in return. She may have had a guy in her life, but something was still missing.

Well Warnings

Take a look at this passage from Psalm 115: "They have mouths but cannot speak; eyes, but they cannot see; they have ears, but cannot hear, noses, but they cannot smell; they have hands, but cannot feel, feet, but they cannot walk; nor can they utter a sound with their throats. Those who make them will become like them and so will all who put their trust in them" (vv. 5-8).

This passage sounds like the definition of a paperdoll, except that it's how the psalmist describes a group of people. Originally, this was an observation about people who had turned away from God, the only Source of perfect love, and instead turned to worshiping their piles of sparkling manmade junk. By turning away from God and trying to fill life with the things they thought mattered, they became paper-like and lifeless. They disengaged emotion from intellect. They disengaged responsibility from action. They were still technically alive, but they had stopped worshiping, loving, serving and giving. They weren't really living at all.

The Israelites fell into the same pattern during their 40-year power walk toward the Promised Land. God was there with them in the wilderness, lighting their path with His fiery presence at night, parting the sea, crushing the armies that came against them, and sending manna from the clouds like a desert snowstorm.

Then they go worship a big ugly cow. What gives?

It seems silly, but we can be guilty of the same thing. An idol is anything or anyone we put in the place of God. When we funnel our heart, mind, soul and strength into finding perfect love and wholeness in anything but God, we become like those people the psalmist described. We tend to become more like what we love. We can become paper and empty, lifeless and listless; or we can become like Christ, compassionate, kind and loving, poised for adventure, ready to walk away from the well and into real life.

The One Who Waits

We've spent all this time imagining Sam going to the well. Now try to imagine the look in Jesus' eyes when she moved toward Him. Jesus knows that women were created to walk as loved, confident, strong, beautiful and compassionate image bearers of

God. Instead, as Sam walked toward the well on that day, He sees a picture of what this woman had become: addicted, defeated, neglected, caught in a string of bad relationships that felt a little bit like love, confused and empty.

And so very thirsty.

There is a beautiful sentence in John 4 just waiting to drip off the page and into a thirsty heart: "[Jesus] *had* to go through Samaria" (v. 4, emphasis added). Technically, Jesus didn't *have* to go through Samaria. He could have gone around it, and it would have been culturally acceptable to do so to a fault. Jesus was Jewish, after all, and the Jewish people wanted nothing to do with Samaritans. Samaria was a volatile area, and the Jews didn't associate with Samaritan people.[2] They wouldn't even drink from the same cup a Samaritan drank from. They went by a separate road—a much longer road—that wound all the way around the area.

But Jesus didn't go around. He had to go to Samaria, so John says, and He went straight through the middle. We know there was a physical reason He stopped by the well that day. He was tired and thirsty. But I believe there was another reason He had to stop: He had to stop for a girl He dearly loved. He stopped for a people He wanted to reach. He was breaking social taboos by sitting there, waiting for her and talking to her. She mattered to Him. How the people in her village saw her didn't matter; what mattered was how *He* saw her. She was worth stopping for. She came just the way she was, and He offered her love that would ricochet through a town and a world through the rest of time.

She was an ordinary girl, but she came face to face with an extraordinary God. She rooted herself in one perfect love. And the wallflower bloomed.

Jesus had no political agenda in Samaria, so He didn't mind associating with a woman who could get Him nowhere. He wasn't ashamed to be near her. At a moment in this woman's life when she was alone and lonely, He met her. The love she'd searched for in the arms of five different men—the love she probably didn't get from the people in her village—all dimmed in light of His love. Jesus' time on earth was short and His mission was urgent, but she was worth waiting for.

That is such a mysterious thing about our Triune God. He spoke a gauzy Milky Way across the night sky and told the stars where to blink. He created sunlight and water and waves. The earth reflects His glory in a stunning way, reminding us of how small and insignificant we really are. And then came Jesus, God in the flesh, who looked people in the eye, spoke to them, ate with them and told them they mattered. More than stars or moonlight or mountain ranges, we matter to Him. He didn't belong in a crummy diseased world like ours, but He came anyway, straight into forbidden territory, to win our heart.

Out of nowhere, love calls the wallflower out on the dance floor. Love asks the unlikely to do something brave. Love sees us watching from far off in the distance and invites us in closer to know Him deeper. Love watches while we cast our nets and meander through our daily lives and asks us to do something more courageous than we ever thought possible. Love sees where we've been rejected and hurt before and sweeps us up into a divine romance.

Love reminds us that we are no longer chained by anonymity. We can walk in the confidence, grace and beauty of a woman who is infinitely loved by the God of the universe. Love gives us a way out of even our darkest sins and obsessions and addictions. Just as we are, right at this nanosecond, we are loved completely and fully by God. We're worth waiting for. We were even worth dying for.

Picture your darkest place of shame or pain. Picture the places you've gone to hoping for acceptance and hope. Then picture Him standing beside it.

Living in the fullness of God is so much better than the wells we keep going to for perfect love. He's it. He is the only perfect love. Trying to dig it up from other places to ultimately fill the deepest longings in our hearts is a colossal waste of time.

Jesus went through forbidden territory to win the heart of a girl He loved. Later when He stretched His arms out on the cross, He again went to forbidden territory, on a vile death march, to win the heart of a girl He loved. And He rose victorious.

You're not forgotten. You're not rejected. You're not just a product of your past. And you are definitely not alone.

Brand New Day

I'm naive in many ways, but I'm old enough know that even a heart primed for passion can be smashed by rejection. Even friends who stand by one minute might bail when life gets too gritty. I'm old enough to know that one poor decision can leave a scar that burns a lifetime.

Being young doesn't mean we're not old enough to have a past, and it certainly doesn't mean we're not old enough to have a list of regrets we wish we could do over. It's too bad that time machines don't exist. I bet you can already think of seasons you would gladly revisit to steer your younger idiotic self in a whole different direction.

But Jesus offers something even more wonderful than a chance at a do-over. He offers us redemption, and that will be the best part of our story when it's all finally written. We have the grace of God raining down over our heart and soul, reminding us this is a new day. The day by the well marked a beginning in Sam's life. She didn't get to go back and correct her mistake, but she could walk free from shame and condemnation.

I think there is one more piece of advice I would bestow on the girl I was back in college, and the girl I am now, and even to you: You aren't plain or forgotten or worthless. It doesn't matter what they say about you, because He says you're worth dying for. He has a message for you: Fall desperately in love with the One who thinks you're more beautiful than a galaxy of stars. Let Him stir your imagination. Let Him fill your heart with forgiveness and freedom. Carry the pieces of your heart to Him and let Him put them back together. Watch Him breathe life back into your broken dreams. Feel the light of a new day and a new beginning move across your face and warm your heart.

Walk away from the well, paperdoll. There is a big life out there for you to live.

Confessions

Father, forgive me for having such a fickle heart.
Forgive me for all the seasons I've chased after false love.
I know better. I know only Your love can truly fill me.
Thank You for giving me the courage to walk in grace
and freedom. I know I don't have to look back in shame
and regret. Thank You for waiting for me by my wells
of my life, for giving me a new beginning, for reminding
me Your perfect love is deeper and more amazing
than I'll ever really understand. As much as I can
in this lifetime, I want to experience that love.
Show me how.

Notes

1. Phillip Yancey, *The Bible Jesus Read* (Grand Rapids, MI: Zondervan, 1999), p. 144.
2. If you're up for a quick history lesson, the riff between the Jews and the Samaritans started when the Assyrians conquered the Northern Kingdom and deported many Jews back into Assyria. Then foreigners were brought in to help keep the peace and work the land. The remaining Jews intermarried with these foreigners, resulting in a "mixed race" called the Samaritans. The "pure" Jews hated this mixed race. See the *Life Application Study Bible, TNIV* (Wheaton, IL: Tyndale, 1996), p. 1627.

3

Beautiful Scars

When a Samaritan woman came to draw water,
Jesus said to her, "Will you give me a drink?"
(His disciples had gone into the town to buy food.)
The Samaritan woman said to him,
"You are a Jew and I am a Samaritan woman.
How can you ask me for a drink?"
(For Jews did not associate with Samaritans.)

JOHN 4:7-9

❀ ❀ ❀

Erin collects seashells. There are hundreds of shell pieces washed up on the
shore today, jagged as broken glass. The sea has handed us a mighty ransom
for our company. I tell her just to pick the special one and then watch her
eyes scrutinize the pile. Her tiny fingers lift one shell from the mix.
I think it will be a sand dollar or one of those conch shells full of ocean—
something beautiful and unique. Instead, she picks up broken pieces, tiny
shell fragments with splashy colors and interrupted swirls.
"Why these?" I ask when she puts them in my hand.
"They're special," she replies.
"They're broken," I say. It comes out more like a question than a statement.
"What makes a seashell special, then?" she asks me.
And it makes me wonder. What does make a seashell special? Is it the size or
shape or color? Or the part that's missing? Or is it something else altogether?
"You do," I finally decide. "When you love something, you make it special."
"Cool," she says. "I like the broken ones."
So we take the broken ones back inside. Erin cleans each piece,
sets it in a perfect row with the rest, and then stands back to marvel
at her handy work. And I marvel too, because suddenly a string
of broken seashells looks more like a diamond necklace some
mermaid flung toward us from the depths of the sea.

❀ ❀ ❀

The room was a stark sanitized white. She lay on the bed, breathing nervously under the blinding lights. Her body was a map of "imperfections"—a guide to help her surgeon to craft her body into the body of an actress whose picture was tacked to the wall. This wasn't a minor cosmetic procedure; this was a major cosmetic overhaul.

I kept my eyes glued to the television set, thinking eventually she would tell them to stop. She was already gorgeous anyway, a classic beauty. It didn't seem to matter. She wanted her face to be changed completely, conformed to the face of her favorite celebrity. She had one goal: to become *that* woman. Her nose would be whittled down and the fat sucked from her cheeks, hips and stomach.

I couldn't help but wonder if she thought having some version of that woman's face and body would give her that woman's life, too. We've all been there (though most of us haven't taken it that far)—we've dreamed of what it might be like to be the woman in the pictures. She seems to have it all: beauty, a boyfriend and red carpet premiers.

I could feel my heart breaking for this girl. She thought beautiful was finally within her reach. She didn't realize beautiful was already her reality. *She'll change her mind,* I thought. *Surely, she'll change her mind. Why would she go through all this when she was already beautiful?* She looked like she was about to speak, but then, instead, she stared at the picture of the woman she'd never met; the image of this paper girl with the perfect body and life. She stared, lifelessly, into the vacant eyes of her paperdoll, willing herself to become like her. And then her eyes fluttered shut.

Pretty Paper Faces

I've never gone through hours of surgery to look like a celebrity, but I've misunderstood what beautiful really looks like, too. For many years, I convinced myself that one of the primary attributes about my body that kept me from being beautiful (an attribute that couldn't be changed) was best summarized by my scars. Models in magazine layouts never have scars. Starlets and sitcom girls seem to be flawless. In my mirror, all I saw was the face of a girl who wanted to be beautiful but felt completely, and utterly, flawed.

Tracing from my hip to my knee on both legs are thick pink imprints; scars from surgeries when I was a little girl. I was born with a rare bone disease called osteogenesis imperfecta. Even though I looked like a normal kid (just small for my age), my bones were fragile. The bone I broke most often was my femur bone, the long bone that connects the hip to the knee, and several surgeries were required to repair it. The scars left over on my thighs are significant—they overlap one another like thick branches. When I was little, I thought they were cool. But by the time I reached 17 and was bombarding my mind with images of perfect women, I was positive that my scars could earn me a one-way ticket into circus freakdom.

It wasn't just that my scars (which few people have ever even seen) made me so self-conscious. It was what those scars represented. I spent most of elementary school and middle school using a wheelchair or a walker. Most of the time I was okay with it, but at other times I couldn't help thinking about this glorious adolescent world I was missing: basketball practice, running, jump rope, actually *dancing* at dances.

Even now as an adult, when I'm supposed to be this confident woman I've always dreamed of becoming, my scars are still there; my own private reminders of my physical weakness. My type of osteogenesis imperfecta is mild, so I haven't had a bone break in several years. I'm not as "fragile" as I used to be. I don't have to use a wheelchair or a walker, and you probably wouldn't notice anything unusual about the way I walk. But my scars remind me I'm different. The imperfections might be covered and veiled underneath years of therapy, but they are still there. I know my body is the polar opposite of a paperdoll's body. And I remember the things people said about it.

One of the scars I think about most—an emotional kind that stuck on my heart for years—came in sixth grade. I was learning to use a walker instead of a wheelchair, and I was en route to the cafeteria. On my way out the door, I heard one snarky girl proudly announce to her friends that I walked like a duck. I felt tears burning in the corners of my eyes. They all giggled, their high-pitched laughs sounding like glass breaking. I don't know why I let it get to me. I had my own great friends who thought I was okay the way I was. I had sweet parents who told me I was adorable. But her voice resonated more clearly than theirs did.

I may not walk like a duck these days, but that girl—who used a walker, and wore hot pink glasses, and kept her nose glued to books—is still the girl I usually see when I look in a mirror. She has better hair now, and somebody told her that wearing puff paint T-shirts every day was not cool (thank goodness), but she's still me. She still hopes she's a little bit beautiful. She still compares herself to other women.

Sometimes, it feels as if there are two different definitions of beauty warring against each other in my mind. One says I walk like a duck and am a bundle of epic imperfections, and therefore "beautiful" is something I will never really be. And then there's this other definition. It's more like a still, soft voice that gently reminds me I'm not made to wallow in this obsession; that I'm not made in the image of some two-dimensional paperdoll. I'm made in the image of a holy God: beautiful. Those two thoughts don't often coexist without turmoil.

It was particularly hard back then.

In my mind, "beautiful" was linked to the external. Scars didn't cover the bodies of all the fictional women I spent so much time reading about; they weren't for the Meg Murrys and Anne Shirleys. In a storybook, scars cover the body of the villain, not the legs of the heroine, and they certainly don't wrap around the legs of models and cover girls.

Paperdolls are never insecure, because every guy wants to date them. Girls want to be them. They are undeniable outer perfection. So what if there's nothing going on beneath the surface? At least they're beautiful.

But who gets to define beautiful anyway? It's a concept that has stumped poets, songwriters and storytellers for decades. It has inspired war and greatness in the same breath. According to paperdoll theology, beauty is really quite simple. It is a shape. It is a jean size. It is a weight, a height, an ethnicity or a race. It is what defines our worth and makes us loveable. It is always something we aren't, but it's close to us, always dangling there in front of our face, begging us to reach a little bit further and take hold of it. And so we start to think, *If I just gave it a little more of my heart, my soul, my mind, my strength . . . it will be me.* What starts as a valid desire so easily trips into full-blown obsession.

The desire we carry in our hearts to be beautiful never goes away. When I talked about scars and beauty at an event recently, an adorable 15-year-old girl came up to talk to me afterward about how the emotional scars in her heart seemed to rip wide open again and again as she made her way through high school. Right behind her, her mom told me that she felt the same way about herself. Even at a gorgeous 40-something, she still struggled with the concept of beauty. How does the pursuit of beauty, which starts out so innocent and normal, end up leaving us so empty?

Since the Samaritan woman's story happened thousands of years ago, she didn't have to stack her worth against magazine girls. In fact, the word "beautiful" is never mentioned in her conversation by the well. But her story is so wrapped in this higher definition of beauty, worth and what it really means to be a woman that we would be crazy to overlook it.

As a society, our definition of beauty is, ironically, flawed. Beauty isn't meant to break our heart and cast us aside. It isn't meant to chain us to disease. It was never intended to be cut into our arms. It was never meant to flash across our minds when we throw up again, or stop eating, or obsess about food, or feed a hunger that never goes away. Beautiful isn't blowing through another credit card or spending 500 dollars on a designer bedazzled tank top. Beautiful is different.

True beauty will change the way we see the world and the way we see ourselves. Beautiful is what we already are, not what we have to die trying to become.

The Samaritan woman has taught me so much about what that word really means. I think she knew how it felt to be broken. And I think she walked away from the well that day beautiful.

Free to Be Beautiful

Sam's culture may be separated from ours in many regards, particularly by time and custom, but it is similar in this: Her culture also had a flawed perception of worth, especially when it came to a woman's worth. Women weren't supposed to be acknowledged or spoken to on the street. A woman was supposed to walk six steps behind her husband.

Education for women was an especially controversial topic in Judaism. An ancient Jewish prayer said, "Thank You, Lord, that I wasn't born a gentile, a dog or a woman." According to custom, women couldn't even learn from a rabbi.

For most women I know, education is a pursuit to which we give much of our heart. We study for what seems like a lifetime, moving through high school and college, trying to cram all this information into a place in our brains where it will actually stay. Then we continue opening our minds and hearts to what's happening in our world and in our universe. Whether it's learning to play a new guitar riff or memorizing the bones in the foot, we all have some kind of intellectual pursuit we want to chase. Most likely, the Samaritan woman wasn't encouraged to pursue knowledge in that way. She didn't live in a society that valued a woman's mind.

Much of a woman's worth and identity in her culture was attached to marriage and bearing children (particularly sons). If you picture passages of the Bible like a movie, some of the most painful scenes to watch (for women at least) are those of single-ness and childlessness. Those two circumstances in a woman's life still hit a strong emotional chord in us. Remember Abraham's wife, Sarah, laughing when she heard that she would have a baby at the age of 90? Remember Hannah sobbing through the book of Samuel, hoping and begging for a son? Remember Zachariah's silence-producing freak-out in the Temple when God told him his wife was expecting? And can you imagine how his elderly wife, Elizabeth, must have felt? When women were childless, it became a place where they not only questioned God's timing but also their worth as a person.

We don't know if the Samaritan woman had kids. We do know that she had a heartbreaking love life, as evidenced by the fact that she'd had five husbands and was living with a man she wasn't married to.

Even though I'm convinced that some Bible women had a steely tenacity I just can't seem to find in myself, I don't think their hearts were so different from yours and mine. Despite all the love they had to give away, they found themselves waiting—sometimes against seemingly insurmountable odds—for God to answer their prayers. They found themselves in a long, painful period of time of waiting for a child. Many found themselves widowed and rejected. They were ostracized because of disease, station in life and past mistakes. And sometimes they were even killed for those things.

Our girl by the well didn't have magazines of paperdolls, but worth was a confusing concept in her life, too. Now that you know a little bit more about her culture and situation, take a look at John 4:9 with new eyes. See if you can hear the surprise in her voice when she answers Jesus' question: "You are a Jew and I am a *Samaritan woman* . . . How can you ask me for a drink?" (emphasis added).

She's nothing but a woman, after all, and a Samaritan at that. She's not from the right family. She didn't make the right decisions. She doesn't run with a popular crowd. She has visible scars, too, not physical ones, maybe, but the deep kind you always feel—the kind of scars that convince you you're worthless and make you feel that you'll never be able to look someone in the eye again. She's no stranger to losing people she loves. She walks in the shadow of rejection. Her life has been full of heartache, not opportunity. When it came to the women in her village, she couldn't compare.

And she was never supposed to. She wasn't created in the image of another woman, and neither are we.

The more effort we put into trying to conform our life to that standard of perfection, the emptier we'll feel and the thirstier we'll become. The story of the woman by the well and the story we are living out in this culture 2,000 years later have a great deal to do with image. Namely this: We aren't made in the image of a paperdoll. We're made in the image of a holy God.

Identity Crisis Solved

In the first chapter of Genesis, God creates a man and a woman in His image. He could have spoken them out of the air and into life, like He did with oceans and stars and mountains, but He didn't. Instead, He formed them; knit together mud and ribs, breath and blood and a beating heart. He knit together a mind and a capacity to love and be loved. He gave them imagination, emotion and choice. People—flawed creatures who laugh and love and breathe and fight and cry and bear all manner of twisted scars—*that* is the part of creation that bears His image. And that is a wonderful mystery to me.

Something about the girl I see in the mirror, the one I gladly pick apart and berate, has the potential to show the world a picture of God's love. When I try to understand that, I find myself asking the same things the Samaritan woman did: *What about me could possibly bear the image of a holy God? What in me is beautiful enough, wild enough and compassionate enough to reflect my Creator?*

It makes me think of my niece, Erin, picking up those broken seashells on the edge of the ocean. Because she wanted them, they became beautiful. Our culture's message seems to be this: becoming beautiful, no matter what it takes, will make us more loved. We see it in almost every advertisement geared toward younger women. In the ad for a pair of jeans, the girl wearing the jeans is locked tight in the arms of a beautiful guy. In the ad for lip gloss, the girl wearing the lip gloss now has the capacity to catch the eye of the guitar player on stage. The truth of the matter is really the reverse: we are already loved, and therefore we are unbelievably, amazingly, beautiful. Jesus stops, waits and pursues us because He loves us, not because of how we look, what we drive or anything else external.

The fashion magazine in my bathroom will give me an entire list of requirements if I let it, and I will never, ever, be able to reach those standards of perfection. God's words are different. They are absolute truth. They can change my life. Which voice will I choose to listen to?

I can conform to a paper culture, or I can follow a God who offers a more appealing option: being *transformed* by the renewing of my mind and heart. I don't have to look at the world like a jaded consumer anymore. I don't have to fish for compliments to fix my own insecurity. I don't have to spend all my effort trying to be another pretty paper face. What Jesus did by the well . . . and what He did later on the cross . . . set me free to be truly, astoundingly, beautiful.

A New Kind of Beautiful

In her wonderful book *Do You Think I'm Beautiful?* Angela Thomas poses three questions: "God, will you fight for me? Will you come for me? Will you say I'm beautiful?" She adds, "I believe that a woman will struggle with trust, hope, and desire until she allows herself to ask these questions and receive the answers from God."[1]

John 4 tells the story of a woman who did exactly that. Her journey to the well can teach us volumes about true beauty.

Jesus Didn't Define Her Worth by Her Gender

Being a woman isn't what keeps us on the outskirts of the world; it's what gives us the unique capacity to change our world. It doesn't matter if we have a sordid reputation or are physically weak. It doesn't matter if we process the world through our heart first and then our mind. Our past doesn't define our worth, and neither do our scars. Wealthy or poor, loud or quiet, we all have an incredible story to live out.

The way Jesus engages this woman, and other women in the gospel, is really spectacular. The way He includes women in His message and ministry marks Him in sharp contrast to other religions. Buddha constantly shunned women in His writings and teachings. In Hinduism, being born a woman is evidence of a failure in a previous life. Confucius didn't have much to say about the fair sex—other than giving them a list of rules they had to obey in subservience to men.

Then there's Jesus . . . who stops to speak to women, who looks them in the eye, who knows they matter infinitely, who includes them in His teachings by using lessons that apply to them specifically. In the gospels, we see women following Jesus from town to town, listening to His teaching and asking questions. We see Him in the home of Mary and Martha, eating dinner and telling stories. We see Him healing a bleeding woman on the streets. We see Him being ministered to by women. And we see Him at the well.

Jesus never taught that our worth as a woman is based on our background, our education, our race, our marital status or our career. We are worthy simply, and amazingly, because of Him. And in Psalm 45:1, God tells us He's enthralled with our beauty.

While I have no doubt you're much more physically beautiful than you realize, the kind of beauty that steals His heart is much deeper than that. It encompasses the internal and the external—your heart, your imagination, your emotion, your intellect, your compassion and your sincerity. He happens to think you're beautiful, worth saving, and worth loving.

Jesus Respected Her Intellectually and Emotionally

There is a song I like called "Mood Rings" by Relient K about a guy's girlfriend who shifts from happy to crazy in the span of a few seconds. "Some days she's Jekyll, some days she's Hyde," sings Matt Theiseen, "but at least she makes a lovely pair."[2]

I know many women who process situations with a discerning eye first. I am not one of them. I process everything through my heart and then, eventually, my mind. I make decisions sometimes based on how I feel or what will make other people happy. When I get excited, I flip out. When I'm upset, it shows. I'm typically in control of my emotions, but sometimes they control me. (On those days, I just hope I make a lovely pair.)

As much as people rant about how emotional we girls can be, I think that's part of what makes us beautiful. In fact, I can't imagine a life (or love) free of some type of emotion. Maybe we're oversensitive at times, but occasionally sensitivity is a perfect companion to passion and determination. I like the fact that Jesus didn't shy away from speaking to a woman whose emotional baggage probably felt even heavier than the jar in her arms. We can bring all of the complicated heart issues we struggle with to Him without fear of being made fun of or hurt. He wants to see the real person, not the one hiding behind a paper mask.

However—and this is equally as exciting—we are not just creatures of emotion. Jesus never stereotyped women as silly and oversensitive. He also valued their minds. We have the capacity to think, to feel, to decide and to choose. Our minds are created to understand and process complex thoughts and concepts.

The conversation at the well covers some deep topics in a short amount of time: questions of purpose, relationships and theology. Jesus doesn't downplay her questions as ridiculous.

He seems calm in His exchange. He is teaching; she is learning, asking questions and processing.

I want to pursue my God and engage my culture with my mind as well as with my heart. I want to study His Word and see how it applies to my circumstances. I want to see how my walk with God illuminates music, art and literature. I want to look at star maps and body charts and remember that God spoke one into existence and knitted the other together with His hands. We don't have to over-spiritualize every corner of academia to have a whole new appreciation of God.

How you are feeling matters to Him. And so does what you are thinking. Jesus respected the woman at the well's ability to love with her heart and her mind. I find that pretty incredible.

Jesus Saw the Weight of Her Oppression and Overcame It

There is another key issue of worth in the Samaritan woman's world that parallels our own. Her worth, to her society, wasn't just wrapped in gender; it was also an issue of prejudice. Most people considered the Samaritans a mixed race (they were part Jew, part Gentile). Jews went in a wide circle around Samaria to avoid being near them.

"Prejudice is a burden that confuses the past, threatens the future and renders the present inaccessible." — Maya Angelou

This isn't the first instance of racial discrimination in the Bible, or the first time history paints a tragic picture of segregation. During Jesus' time on earth, He adamantly broke down racial and social barriers, reminding us we are all equal image bearers of God. Even now, in a bold new century hallmarked by technology and new thinking, the issue of race can carve a deep scar into the heart of a young woman.

In 1950, Elliot Erwin snapped what would become an iconic photograph depicting America's struggle with racial injustice. The image shows two different water fountains for two different skin tones, as if skin color were a reason to degrade another person—another image bearer of God. That picture stands as a reminder of one of the most grisly periods of American history. It also illustrates just how racial prejudice and discrimination stand in complete opposition to the message of the gospel.

In this story by the well, Jesus compares His love to a fountain and makes it a point to say that there is only one fountain—only one Source of Living Water—and that water is available for every man and woman. God chose to lock His image in people of all races, nationalities and skin tones. F.B. Meyer pens that heroism this way: "In Him is neither Jew nor Gentile. His Gospel, like bread, water, spring flowers, love, is independent of race."[3]

The physical features, skin tones and body types indigenous to our racial heritage only add to our unique beauty. It in no way diminishes it.

Jesus Saw Beyond Her Questions to Her Deepest Need

Sometimes I have a difficult time trying to communicate what is really on my heart. My parents may not understand what I'm trying to say. My friends may not understand. The guys in my life don't understand. (When it comes to the myriad of ways women try to explain themselves without really explaining anything, my brother likes to issue this reminder: "I don't speak estrogen.") Good grief, sometimes I don't think I even know what I'm trying to say. Trying to articulate struggles with loneliness, desire or beauty is especially hard to explain.

With Jesus, I don't have to stumble around for the right words. He wants an authentic relationship with me. And He sees my real need. Even when I don't get immediate answers to the questions I ask Him (and I ask a *lot* of questions), I know He's looking deeper even than that. He sees my deepest desire for love and acceptance and wants to fill it.

By the well, Jesus immediately answered the woman's question, but He did it in a way that pointed back to her need. Her life, as she's living it, is not working. Jesus offers an alternative: life abundant that will change her world.

Jesus Revealed His Identity as the Son of God to Her First

Just in case we have any doubts about how much Jesus valued this woman, there's one final point we need to make. Up to this point in Jesus' ministry, He hadn't specifically stated that He was the Messiah. People insinuated as much. His disciples probably figured it out. But He hadn't actually said it.

Until now.

The first time He declares His identity as the Promised Messiah is to the Samaritan woman. If you were standing on the road from the well to the village that day, she would have bowled you over like a marathon runner shouting these words: "Come and meet the man who knew everything I ever did."

A bit later on, if you were standing on the path from the tomb where Jesus was buried to the city of Jerusalem, you would have been bowled over by three more women shouting this message: "He is risen!" Not only did Jesus reveal His identity as the Messiah to the woman at the well, but also women just happened to be first at the tomb on resurrection morning.

Jesus entrusted women to carry life-altering, earth-shattering messages into the world. And for us girls on the other side of the well 2,000 years later, He still gives us a message to carry. He still offers us the opportunity to know Him—as friend *and* as savior. Once we realize we are known deeply and loved fully, we no longer have to succumb to paperdoll standards of worth. We can become a whole new radiant definition of what beauty really is.

Beauty Redefined

My heart knows that beauty—the real kind that threads from my heart to my soul to my mind, binding itself to the external—

is possible. Real beauty is quirky and timeless, elegant and artsy. It's in a face full of freckles and in long Spanish braids and in a hard bicep or a soft stomach. It shines bright and breathtaking from a classic girl who wears pearls and stilettos and reads Kate Chopin. It blasts like a rock song from the funky girl on the fringe with blue hair and dark glasses and a collection of Bob Dylan records. It's wrapped in introversion and extroversion, caught in the lilt of an accent.

Beauty isn't some pinpoint we're all shooting for aimlessly. Real beauty is more like a kaleidoscope, shining out of every part of our lives. It is evidenced in thousands of skin tones and smiles, illuminated even from the heart of a girl who sees herself as nothing out of the ordinary. We can't let the pursuit of paper beauty become our obsession. It will only leave us wanting.

There is a deeper kind of beautiful I want to be: I want to be beautiful like my Aunt Ruth, whose kindness and passion (and gorgeous art) makes me feel loved and inspired. Or like my Aunt Lillie, whose spunky sweetness makes me feel at home. I want to be beautiful like my sister: assertive, encouraging and passionate about her life and family. When she talks about doing surgery, I wish I'd gone to medical school, too (which is ironic, as the sight of a paper cut makes me want to throw up).

I want to be beautiful like my friend Marie, who went home to the Lord at a dazzling 87 years of age. Right up until the end, Marie lived life intentionally. She served her church in a decade when it was 6 people around a wood-burning stove, and she served her church 60 years later when there were hundreds of people sitting in the pews. Faithfulness like that is so rare. I want to be beautiful like my friend Heidi. She has osteogenesis imperfecta as well, though hers is a more severe version than mine. I saw some pictures of her at school dance that were fabulous: she looked gorgeous (as always) in a cute dress and a chic short haircut. She was dancing with her friends, crutches and all.

I want to be beautiful like Caitlyn, who spends all week in class and her weekends helping out with a student ministry. I want to be beautiful like my best friend, Melanie, who spends her days engaging the imaginations of adorable fourth graders and then spends the rest of nights hanging out with her adorable twins. Those girls keep giving love whether or not they receive love in return. I want to be beautiful like my mom, who sees the good in people and brings out the best in a person. I want to be beautiful like Erin, who listens to country music while she paints masterpieces, fearlessly takes up for people being picked on, and picks up broken seashells just because they're beautiful.

All those women are more than just pretty. They have different dreams and passions and are at totally different places in their lives, but they have something in common: God's love shines so brightly from their hearts, it takes my breath away. They live like they are loved.

The world is full of pretty paperdolls who dress alike, talk alike and spend 16 hours a day trying to be more physically attractive. Far more rare is a woman who is beautifully *real*, who wraps her worth in the truth of God's Word and carries His love out into the world. I want to be that kind of beautiful.

I'll always light up when somebody tells me that I'm pretty. I want to present the world the best version of me. I just don't want it to be my obsession. Beautiful: heart, mind, soul and strength. Those four ways that God tells us to love Him are internal qualities that have outward ramifications. The Samaritan woman didn't change clothes or lose weight or get a physical makeover on her way back into town after she talked with Jesus, but her transformation was incredible. It literally changed her world. She walked toward the well thirsty and searching. She walked away full and loved. I bet she never looked more beautiful than she did on her way back from the well that day.

We're beautiful broken people who bear the image of a holy God; ordinary girls who have fallen in love with an extraordinary Creator. Let's give Him room to pick up the broken pieces.

Peace in the Scars

Just so you know, most of the time, I'm okay with my scars. In fact, I'm starting to see them as pretty cool.

I'm sure I'll always struggle to some degree with the idea of beauty and self-worth. I'll always be relearning what it means; always processing that beauty is more than what people see. The more I dig into God's Word, the more I believe it, but even then there are days I forget.

Recently, I was walking on the treadmill when I noticed myself in one of the long mirrors. I almost fell off. I was wearing workout shorts, and so, of course, I could see my scars. I felt the heat of paranoia rush from my head to my Asics. What if someone else saw them? What if the guys who grunt and scream when they lift the two-ton barbells looked over and saw my scars? I left soon after, paranoid and panicky, going through my mental checklist of why my body was flawed and gross.

That night I read about Thomas, the infamous doubter of John 20. He wouldn't believe the disciples when they told him that his friend Jesus, who had just been executed in a horrific and gruesome way, was alive. He told them that until he touched the scars in Christ's hands for himself, he wouldn't believe it was all true.

Then along came Jesus, holding out His scarred hands for His dear friend Thomas to see and touch. This was the resurrected Jesus, in a new body not mangled or broken or bound by earth. I thought about how odd that was—that His scars should still be there, ugly scars on His beautiful hands—but that story helped me make peace with my scars. Suddenly, I began to understand that my worth as a person, or as a woman, wasn't wrapped in *my* scars but in *His*. I was enough to die for. No scar I have, on my legs or on my heart, will ever match the pain, ridicule or betrayal Jesus faced on the cross for me. No scar I have will even come close to the scars He still bears on His hands. *He kept His scars for me.*

Because Jesus is God, I know He could have decided not to keep His scars, but He did. And if our scars—the ones on the outside that mark our body or the ones on the inside that mark our heart—remind us of a season in our lives when He was present, a time we know He was with us, how can they not be beautiful as well?

Our physical and emotional scars are nothing to be despised if they represent a time in our lives when God walked us through to wholeness. Even if our scars were caused by something that we did, we shouldn't let them be a source of shame or embarrassment. We serve a God who sees every tear and every scar and makes our pain His pain. We serve a God who heals from the inside out. Even scarred, broken and limping around as these imperfect creatures, we still somehow bear the image of God. His glory is reflected in creation, but His *image* is reflected in *us*, in our hearts, in our lives, even in our scars.

I was still thinking about this when I went to sleep that night—about how Jesus kept His scars for me. Before I fell asleep, I touched the ones on my sides and traced them with my index finger. Suddenly, the picture I'd had for years in my mind's eye —the one of having long pink ugly scars—was replaced. There was no more Frankenstein, no more disfigured villain, no more twisted flaw. The scars were still there, of course, but they don't look the same to me anymore. When I pictured Jesus' scars and then pictured mine, something changed.

I no longer imagined my scars as being ugly, like I was a monster pieced and stitched together. Suddenly, they were curling and blooming onto a canvas—thorns at first, and then roses. They were a winding staircase into a secret tower. Instead of being long brands and labels, they curved and became the perfect papery imprint on a butterfly's wing. And when those wings hit the sunlight, they looked like a painting.

Suddenly, they were beautiful.

Confessions

Lord, ever so slowly, I'm starting to see the girl
You see when You look at me. When other people look
at me, whether they see my smile or my scars, I want them
to see You. Make something beautiful out of my broken heart.
Help me find beauty in broken, unlikely places. I'm tired of
fixing my mind and heart on the image of a paperdoll;
a standard I will never ever meet. Instead, help me to fix my
eyes on You. Your beauty takes my breath away.

Notes

1. Angela Thomas, *Do You Think I'm Beautiful?* (Nashville, TN: Thomas Nelson Publishers, 2003), p. 17.
2. Relient K, "Mood Rings," from the album *Two Lefts Don't Make a Right* (Gotee Records, 2003).
3. F.B. Meyer, *The Life of Love* (Old Tappan, NJ: Revell, 1987), p. 89.

4

Waiting for Gilbert

He told her, "Go, call your husband and come back." "I have no husband," she replied. Jesus said to her, "You are right when you say you have no husband. The fact is, you've had five husbands, and the man you now have is not your husband. What you have just said is quite true."

JOHN 4:16-18

Love makes your soul crawl out from its hiding place.

ZORA NEALE HURSTON

I knew I would love him the first time I saw him.

I know what people say about love at first sight . . . that it's not *really* love, it's just an emotional response; that it's a fluke of my girly nature I can blame on pheromones or something like that. But I was certain I had proven the critics wrong. This guy was handsome. He was smart. He was strong and charming; confident without being a jerk about it. I loved him.

And, I was certain, had he been real, he would have loved me back.

His name was Gilbert Blythe, and he was the mere figment of L.M. Montgomery's glorious imagination. His claim to fame was pretty simple: He fell in love with a red-headed writer named Anne Shirley. From the time that they were kids (who couldn't stand each other) to young adults (when they couldn't stand being apart), you couldn't help but root for the two of them to be together.

It was the way he loved her that won me over. He loved her even though she wasn't the prettiest girl. He loved that she was a writer. Her imagination could get out of control, but he found it endearing, not weird. He was willing to make sacrifices so her dreams could come true. When I saw their love story play out on my television, I couldn't stop smiling. There was something about the way he looked at her, and touched her face, and tucked her hair behind her ear, that gave me goose bumps. He was completely taken with her.

Gilbert was no lovesick pushover, though. The two of them argued. They made each other laugh. He challenged her to pursue her dreams. Maybe that's why their love story was so sweet to me: something about their relationship seemed like it could be real.

At approximately the age of 12—with hot pink glasses on my face, a tattered copy of *Anne of Green Gables* in my lap and the movie on virtual repeat in my VCR—I made a pivotal decision about my future love life. No matter how long it took me to find him, I would wait for a Gilbert. I convinced myself that there was some version of him out there, somewhere, thinking about me, too. I decided I would save all of my heart for him.

High school raised a whole new crop of insecurities in my heart. When I started feeling lonely, or when I found myself roseless on Valentine's Day, I thought about my "Gilbert" again. Gilbert became my rally cry when I felt invisible or when I got tired of waiting and hoping. It even became a code word between me and my parents. If a guy was godly, funny and handsome (and there was a wide margin of what was considered handsome)—he was a Gilbert.

It was in college that Gilbert really crossed my mind, though, because like most girls, college was when I started thinking about what kind of man I wanted to marry. I knew I wanted him to love the Lord. He wouldn't just do church on Sundays because he felt he had to. His love for God would show in his life, his words and the way he treated people. Integrity would matter more to him than popularity. He would have a quiet kind of confidence about him. He would be able to make me laugh. I wanted him to be a dear friend to me, too—a kindred spirit, as Anne would say. We could pray together and talk about God, music, movies and love, all in the same conversation. But he wouldn't *just* be another guy friend I could high-five and rent movies with. He would look at me as if he were truly in love with me. He would hold my hand for no reason. And he would be an amazing kisser.

I dared to believe he was out there somewhere, so I kept hoping and I kept waiting. I prayed for him sometimes, which always felt a little awkward (because I didn't know his name), but also somehow felt so right. Waiting felt worth it then. I was already in love with him, I decided. I just didn't know who he was yet.

Of all the thousands of ways we girls are different, lost in our own quirky dreams and hopes, we seem to have at least one thing in common: we want to fall in love. Love is the one risk we're all willing to take.

I've never been a throw-caution-to-the-wind kind of girl. I stay away from bungee jumping and skydiving and anything else that might elicit an immediate vomit reflex. But I think falling in love is similar to a freefall. Real love involves transparency and trust. It's a decision to love even when I'm angry and upset, to guard another person's reputation fiercely, to respect another person, to offer so much of my heart. It's terrifying as much as it is beautiful. And it's a risk I'm willing to take. Romance is one of the strongest desires in my heart—the one that never really goes away with time or maturity.

I think we're all waiting to lock eyes with someone who is crazy about us; someone who calls us beautiful, who gives us the boost we need to catch our craziest, most far-off dreams. We hope, and pray, he's out there somewhere.

I've learned, though, that what starts as a pure dream and hope—what starts out as a journey to a happily ever after—often ends by the well.

Heart-shaped Paradigm

Ironically (or maybe not so ironically), I'm sitting here writing about love and longing at a breakfast nook at the beach—alone. Nothing beats coming to the pier and asking for a table for one. To make matters worse, I'm surrounded by cute couples.

If I were here with a guy, I think my perspective on this place would be different. If I were here with my Gilbert, I might describe this as a romantic little beach café. I would point out the checkered print on the tablecloth and the baskets of red daisies hanging in the windows. I might tell you that he and I split some French toast and laughed about the shell-shaped ashtrays in the shop next door. But I'm here alone. So today, this is just a funky little breakfast nook on the pier. And there is a fly buzzing around my half-eaten French toast that is driving me crazy.

Love changes how I look at my life, too. It becomes this paradigm for how I view every decision, dream and relationship. I'm learning that when I choose to love someone, be it as friends or romantically, that decision affects everything I do and say. Nothing can compare to walking with the confidence of a girl who is loved. When love (or some cheap imitation of it) leaves me broken, rejection permeates my actions, hopes, words and dreams. It spreads across my heart like an ink stain, blotting away my confidence.

Sometimes, it takes a relationship ending for us to see that we've become somebody's paperdoll—a version of a girl we thought he might like, but who is really nothing like the girl inside. We've taken up all his hobbies. We've worn what we thought he would want us to wear. We changed everything for his love—our hair, our clothes, our major, our interests. We learn it is very possible (and sometimes very easy) to love someone who won't love us back. Under the paper shell of the girl we used to be lurks an awful truth we hope no one sees: we are terrified of being unwanted. So we keep tossing out our hearts, hoping that someday they won't come hurling back toward our face bruised and wasted. In the name of love, we make some dangerous compromises.

For those of us with bruised hearts and pretty paper smiles, one of the biggest lessons by the well is about to hit close to home. *Love* is the breaking point in the Samaritan woman's journey. She *may* have been struggling with many things that day, but Jesus brought up one specific issue that attached itself to her spiritual longing: her love life.

Jesus doesn't embellish or downplay the facts. He knows she's been wounded from past love and mentions this (see John 4:18). He also knows that she is presently living with a man who isn't her husband, and He mentions this, too. Her heart was wide open there in His presence, and He saw the pain and the frustration giving her heart away had caused.

He looked at her heart first. That had to be something to behold if you were the Samaritan woman: a Jewish man who looked past pretense and public opinion—who looked deeper than a paper smile—into the most broken pieces of her heart. That had to be an incredible realization. He didn't just see her past, or her living situation, or what she looked like, or even where she was from. He really saw her—her pain, her sorrow, her joy. Everything.

The pain in our hearts that comes from longing for romance is no secret to Him, either. In all this chasing and searching and praying and hoping, He sees the desires we have to be loved. He sees our longing for just one guy to pick us out, say we're special, and tell us we matter. He knows the pain that comes from rejection. He knows the myriad of ways a heart can be kicked around, but He is also the giver of all good and beautiful things. He offers real hope that can pull us through this longing; answers that contrast our culture in some significant ways.

Our paperdoll world seems to offer a varied definition of true romance and love: casual sex, weekend hookups and friendships that are sometimes more than friendships—all of which leave us emotionally drained. My culture often suggests that sex outside of marriage has no negative consequences. It insinuates that we're only driven by feeling and impulse.

If you take a 10-minute drive down the interstate or look at the back of almost any woman's magazine, you will typically see a paperdoll advertising some product and linking it to the physical. She is seductively confident as she stares off the page or billboard, all in an effort to sell a purse or pack of gum or a bag of frozen French fries. The subtle message is sometimes not so subtle at all: your body is a tool to get what you want.

Sam's story by the well can help us untangle all of these touched-up lies and start processing a deeper truth. In my own life, I'm learning that falling in love—even at its best and most amazing, even with some modern-day shaggy-haired Gilbert— will never complete me. It will definitely add to the beauty of my life, but there isn't a guy who can fill my deepest longing to be loved.

I'm learning that God's forgiveness is real, beautiful and true, even for boundaries I've crossed.

I'm learning to take my whole messy heart to God. He knows how much love matters to me and how much just the thought of it moves me. He knows His timing confuses me, but He's ready to help me walk through this season with my heart intact. And I'm learning He asks me to keep physical boundaries in my relationships with guys for a reason. There's a reason He wants me to wait.

I'm learning to let the Author of romance really define the word for me and, much like Sam, I'm learning that His love is more deep, beautiful, and wonderful than I ever realized.

Every Last Corner of My Heart

I was walking along my college campus around Valentine's Day one year when I spotted a bizarre message scribbled in pale pink chalk on the sidewalk: "Jesus is my boyfriend."

I suddenly felt very immature and unspiritual. I do love Jesus. I want to experience the fullness of God in my life. I want to engage Him at every opportunity while I'm walking on this earth. But it was Valentine's Day and, so help me, I just wanted a mixed CD and a bundle of daisies from a sweet guy. I want to fall in love, too. I started to wonder if those two longings could coexist.

When it comes to how much God cares about our love lives, I see two different (but dangerous) myths on just how involved we think He wants to be. The first myth is that we should never, ever, long for true love if we're living in the fullness of Christ. Romance shouldn't be an issue if we're tight with God.

That mentality will only break our hearts. God created man and woman to fall in love. He thought of romance, and hand holding, and a first kiss. He gave us the capacity to love in many different ways. He tucked that desire deep inside of us. Because He is a good God, I don't think He did that to break our hearts. I think He gave us that longing for a reason. He confirms over and over in His Word that His plans for our lives are good plans; that He is for us, not against us. The Bible is full of gorgeous love stories. God is enough, for certain, and His love is the only one that can truly make us whole. But longing for romance isn't a result of spiritual immaturity; it's what happens to humans who love deeply. Romance, when it's real, adds to the beauty.

The second myth is that we can follow God without involving Him in our love lives. We might give Him most of our hearts—the part that houses the big decisions and hopes for the future—but not the part we're secretly hoping some Gilbert will find and keep. We try to answer all these questions about sexuality with books and magazines and talk shows and advice from friends who seem to know what they're talking about, but we never look at what God has to say about the issue in His Word.

Some of the rockiest times in my faith have come when I have tried to segregate my life into holy places and common places—when I've tried to break off what is "spiritual" from the rest of my life, when really there should be no separation. God wants *every corner* of our hearts. Sometimes, the walk to the well is a long one. It may begin when we pour out more and more of our hearts over the phone. It may begin on an instant message, where it's easy to be a little bit wittier and disclose more than we would in person. Most girls I know (myself included) tend to attach to a guy emotionally long before they attach to one physically.

In her book *Every Woman's Battle,* Shannon Ethridge writes:

> By definition our sexuality isn't what we do . . . our sexuality is who we are and we were made with a body, mind, heart, and spirit, not just a body. Therefore sexual integrity isn't just about physical chastity. It is about purity in all four aspects of being.[1]

God tells us in His Word that sex is reserved for marriage. Yielding our desire for romance to His Lordship is hard, but it's also liberating. Jesus proves this to our girl by the well. Sam is really interested in this concept of "living water." Take a look at their conversation again: "The woman said to him, 'Sir, give me this water so that I won't get thirsty and have to keep coming here to draw water' " (John 4:15). Jesus' answer seems rather bizarre: "Go, call your husband and then come back" (v. 16).

I wonder if she raised an eyebrow at this. I mean, really, what did her *husband* have to do with living water? She's talking water, worship, and theology here—not guys. But Jesus didn't just see her heart in pieces; He knew that everything connected. He knew what she'd done in the past. He knew that her heart was suffocating, even when she was with another man. He wanted access to every part of her heart, and He offered her a healing, and wholeness, that no man would ever be able to offer.

Really Bad Love Stories

If Sam could sit down across from us and tell us about her life, five different love stories would emerge.[2] We would hear how she met her five husbands. We might even hear the hopes and dreams she had for their lives together. What we wouldn't hear is a happily ever after. Somehow, every relationship led to the same place: a deep dark well.

When it comes to guarding our own hearts and minds, I can think of a few ways in particular we end up on a fast trek to the well, hoping that romance will satisfy the longing for love in our hearts that only God can fill.

1. We Let Physical and Emotional Barriers Crumble

Picture two girls at a large student gathering. Girl #1 has a boyfriend whom she is, obviously, crazy about. Wherever he goes, she goes, and you wonder for a minute if maybe they really are attached somehow. She keeps her finger hooked onto his belt loop when he walks. When he talks to someone else, she stands close to him, eying this other individual (glaring if this individual is female). As the speaker shares his message, this girl keeps tracing her thumb across her boyfriend's hand, or putting her head on his shoulder, or scooting closer so that her seat is mostly vacant. Affection is one thing, but it would probably be safe to assume that keeping up physical and emotional boundaries in this relationship is going to get more and more difficult.

Now picture Girl #2. She has a boyfriend, too, but she seems to be confident doing her own thing. She's not insecure when he socializes with people. She's a little bit guarded physically around him. She holds his hand. She puts her arm through his when he walks, but she is aware of how easy it is to let physical barriers crumble. Because she cares so much for him, she exercises some self-control.

Self-control is really difficult. Lauren Winner wrote a book called *Real Sex*, which is incredible for so many reasons. She's a great writer, and she graciously admits that the entire concept of chastity is one she's struggled against a great deal in her Christian walk. I related immediately to her honesty because, quite frankly, chastity seemed much more romantic and do-able when I was younger.[3] As I meandered through my twen-ties, it still seemed romantic, but also frustrating. There's a part of my heart always ready to argue this one; always ready to grumble about rules. C.S. Lewis said, "Christianity seems at first to be all about morality, all about duties and rules and guilt and virtue, yet it leads you on, out of all that, into some-thing beyond."[4] I like that thought. I like knowing that God is telling me to wait for a reason, and the reminder that antic-ipation is something to be savored, too.

Physical restraint is a conscious decision. If we don't set—and keep—physical boundaries in our relationships with guys, the boundaries become more and more blurred. Our commit-ments weaken. We push a physical relationship further, justi-fying each new step, giving away more of our body—and our heart—than we ever thought we would.

As overwhelming as the compulsion is to touch, kiss and hold each other, there's kind of an odd irony here: the longer the anticipation builds, the more we learn to experience (and appreciate) just how deep real love is. It would be enough to save sex until I'm married just because God said so. But I think maybe He says so for a sweet reason: so that the expe-rience will be amazing. In that context, we can offer all of ourselves to someone who has promised, before God, to love us forever.

Think about how many people point to Jane Austen as the reigning queen of romance writing. There was no blatant sex in her books; romance was the hallmark of each of her sto-ries. Her love-struck heroes and heroines had to focus on something besides just physicality. Edward and Fitzwilliam and all those other handsome guys in top hats and coattails had to work to win the *hearts* of the women they loved.

The women in these stories exercised a mighty power in the presence of these men: self-control. Sometimes in the movies based on these books you can almost feel the tension coming off the screen, but the restraint they show makes the love even more wonderful. The guy doesn't just love her for her body; he loves *her*.

I want to be loved like that. I don't want to give another piece of my heart, or my body, to a guy who isn't committed to me permanently. The apostle Paul gives more love advice in Ephesians. He tells husbands to love their wives like Christ loved the church (see Eph. 5:25). Jesus was willing to lay down His life for the church. He saw it at its best and worst and thought it was incredible and worth loving. He saw something distinctly beautiful about it. He knew its potential and spoke of that potential with passion. I want that kind of love. I'm willing to wait for that, and I want to give as much of myself as I can give to one guy. My friend Lisa says that setting boundaries isn't just an issue of knowing how far is too far, but knowing how much she can save. That kind of romance reflects the nature of a holy God who writes incredible love stories.

God isn't asking us to wait on His timing to keep us from experiencing good. He is asking us to wait so we can experience something amazing. This isn't some boring wait, like a wait at the drive-through. Waiting for God's best is like the final moment of silence before the symphony starts, or the second just before sunrise.

2. We Wrap Our Worth in the Guy Holding Our Hand

I went to high school during a dark time of history when cell phones were merely tracking devices. We had them, but we were only allowed to use them during emergencies *or else*. Text messaging did not exist. A phone with Internet access never even crossed our mind—that was far too futuristic. On the bright side, we had to actually look another person in the face when we talked to him or her and make conversation. With no cell

phones and no texting, communication during class time had
to be done in the same manner as our short attention spanned
forefathers: by passing notes.

One day, I noticed a note lying in front of my locker. My
friend and I immediately reached for it, even though we knew
the loopy cursive writing wasn't ours. (I tried to rationalize a
noble reason why we picked the note up, but really, we were just
nosy.) One sentence stood out above the rest: *If I do this, maybe
he'll stay.*

If we get to that point in our relationships—the point where
we try to think of something else to do so he'll stay—we might
as well be camping out by the well. Love you have to manipulate from a person isn't love at all.

3. We Think Every Guy Should be a Chick-flick Hero

Until I started working in student ministry, I didn't know this
very obvious thing about guys: they're insecure, too. They think
about us as much as we think about them. As much as we feel
picked over sometimes for girls who are prettier and more attractive, guys feel that way, too. And as a student ministry
worker, I couldn't help but scratch my head more than once at
some genuinely amazing guys whom girls didn't seem to be
into. The genuinely kind guy was "just a friend." And that
makes me kind of sad.

It seems that so many women, regardless of age, are prone
to get a little too wrapped up in a fantasy world. Guys in books
and movies always say the right things; and that's because they
are completely fiction. Life isn't nearly as cliché or predictable
as a movie, and guys aren't perfect. And that's good to know,
because I'm not perfect either. Perfection is best left to cheesy
movies. Just the fact that two ordinary people can fall in love in
such a broken world is pretty incredible to me.

Even though I say I'm waiting for a "Gilbert," I also know
that Gilbert is fiction. I'm not looking for someone who doesn't
exist. Loving someone completely—imperfections, weaknesses

and all—is what makes real love better than storybook love. We should be choosy when it comes to important things we're looking for in another person: whether he loves God (and shows it in his life), how he respects you, and how he respects his family. But we've got to show guys some grace. We shouldn't get so caught up in movie and book characters that we overlook some genuinely wonderful guys.

4. We Allow Bitterness and Defeat to Permeate Our Hearts
I think I represent possibly the smallest faction of women in the United States: I graduated from a Christian college without an engagement ring. In the spring of my senior year, diamonds were as thick on campus as dogwood blossoms. Suddenly, everybody was engaged. Or talking about getting engaged. Or writing moody love songs about how they'd found "the one." I went to college to get a degree, not a ring, but the collective glint radiating from all the sparkly rocks on campus stirred some self-doubt. A few years later, the magic age when I thought I would get married came . . . and went. Gilbert was still MIA. Instead of waiting in anticipation, I started waiting in a constant state of grudgy bitterness.

Waiting *is* hard. It gets terribly lonely sometimes. It's hard to sit in church with young couples and cute families and wonder why life feels so ill-timed. Some days, I remember that God has a specific purpose for my life, right now, just as I am. I funnel all this longing into serving people. I travel and write and live intentionally and love my life. Other days, I go paper. I get bitter and cranky. As I try hard to become some other girl I think *he* might like, I overlook what God is doing in my life right now. I try to hide my loneliness from Him, thinking that if He sees my real desire, He will dangle love in front of me and then take it away.

That mentality is what I call "Monkey's Paw Theology." In high school, I read a short story by W.W. Jacobs called "The Monkey's Paw." In the tale, people wind up with a cursed foot of a monkey (gross, right?) that grants their wishes. The wish comes true, but only in some horrific and twisted kind of way. Some people get that same image of God in their minds. They believe that if they run to Him in their loneliness and tell Him about it, or tell Him some of their deepest dreams and desires, He'll make them wait even longer to find someone—just because He can. Monkey's Paw Theology says that if we confess a fear—of growing old, or not getting into this college, or losing someone we love—God will use that information against us.

I refuse to believe God created the world and then sent His Son to redeem it just so He could mess with our minds and hearts like a vindictive puppet master in the clouds. Remember: He is for us, not against us. He wants the best for us. I don't know the mind of God, and I don't pretend to. I will never understand why He allows certain things to happen. This long journey home seems to be wrapped in confusion as much as mystery. But I refuse to let my enemy, or my paper culture, convince me that God doesn't care about every part of my life. I know that my dreams and desires are safe with Him. There is no one else I want to keep my heart except Him. One of the most dangerous mentalities I see in teen girls, college girls and women in general (especially the woman in my mirror) is that a season of singleness (however long it lasts) somehow points to worthlessness. Or something they've done wrong.

Sam would get how easy it is to let our hearts sink into defeat. If any woman in history had a right to be walking in bitterness, it was the Samaritan woman. She had somehow lost *five* men, which would make any girl reclusive and bitter. I wonder if love was starting to lose its meaning to her, too, just as it does in our culture. In storybooks, the prince kisses the girl and stays by her side forever.

In our not-so-fairy-tale reality, a grimy kingdom of hook ups and hangovers, people say "I love you" and then leave the next day. Love isn't just a word abused by the guys we've known, either. Sometimes parents leave. Sometimes friends leave. But

God's love is not the same as human love. God says He loves us with an everlasting love (see Jer. 31:3). He doesn't just write a happily-ever-after for the beautiful princess who had it all, but also for the girl with the twisted tiara, the girl who fell down broken, or rejected, or picked over. In His kingdom, that girl gets an ever-after as well.

So don't lose heart.

You don't have to sink into bitterness and defeat. You can take your heart to Him and trust, and trust, and trust. You don't serve a God who doesn't understand the meaning of love; you serve a God who writes tremendous love stories out of bad endings, rejection and mistakes.

Why I Am "that Girl"

A common refrain so many women seem to say after a moment of weakness goes something like this: "I didn't think I was 'that kind of girl.'"

The truth is, any of us can easily be "that kind of girl." By the grace of God, I'm still waiting, but I know how easy it would be for me to give myself away, or give pieces of my heart away. I know what my boundaries are. I know that God says to save sex for when I'm married. I have women in my life who keep me accountable in my relationships. But I know how easy it would be to give in to desire. I know I'm *that* girl. My sins are different, but they are no better.

In one of her poems, Madeleine L'Engle writes, "My sins, I fear, dear Lord, lack glamour."[5] Sam would get that. That's the definitive crossover between her culture and ours. She has a guy in her life. She's giving him all of her. But something is still missing. Her heart is still suffocating.

Her quest for a pure love ended beside a lonely well.

Most of us know what it's like to be that girl, standing unglamorous and defeated in our sins. We sign cards and make commitments but still give away too much physically and emotionally. We may lie, manipulate or steal to get what we want. Jealousy eats away at our motives like bright green mold. Jesus seeks us out anyway. His grace gives us all equal footing.

We masquerade as paperdolls sometimes, so afraid people will see what we are really like. What if people knew our sin? What if people knew all about us, just like they did with the Samaritan woman?

So, what if they do? Our worth isn't defined by our past; it's wrapped in Jesus Christ. There is always forgiveness in His arms for every area where we've gone too far.

Jesus mentioned the Samaritan woman's sin, but He didn't do so to condemn or judge her. He did so to shed the light of His merciful love down on her paper world and offer her a love that was real and good and true and better than anything she ever had, or would, experience.

Forgiveness waits by the well and offers a new beginning.

"As far as the east is from the west, so far has he removed our transgressions from us" (Psalm 103:12).

Take My Heart

I hear women talk about the "type" of guys they're attracted to fairly often. Physically, I've never had a type. I'm attracted to guys who look very different from one another. But I still pray for my Gilbert. Even though I'm pretty sure I have no clue what he looks like, what he eats for breakfast or what his favorite kind of music is, I think I know something about his heart. To my best ability, this is how I would describe my type: He is passionate about his relationship with God. He doesn't have to be in seminary or know how to conjugate Greek verbs; I just want to see his love for his Lord in the way he lives. He's the kind of guy who is kind to his mom and his family. He is kind to people who can do nothing for him. God's Word anchors his life, and he is passionate about living intentionally.

> "But with you there is forgiveness; therefore you are feared. I wait for the Lord, my soul waits, and in his word I put my hope. My soul waits for the Lord more than watchmen wait for the morning" (Psalm 130:4-6).

He'll make me laugh and make me smile, and he'll point out beautiful things about life I might glance over. I think he'll know what it's like to get lost in a worship song. He'll have a quiet confidence, and he'll want to be respected more than he wants to be popular.

He will see the good in people. He'll make me want to be the best version of myself—not because he's picky or jerky or insecure (or insincere), but because he lives with passion and purpose. He'll challenge me to pursue my dreams. He'll stand beside me when I'm afraid. His face is the one that will fill up my mind when I tell my future grandkids about the man who stole my heart and why he was worth waiting for.

Much like Gilbert, he'll fall in love with a quirky, sometimes overly passionate freckle-faced writer. I think he'll reach over and hold my hand for no reason. And I think he'll be a great kisser.

But even when Gilbert is in my life (assuming he already isn't), there's a part of my heart even he won't be able to touch. I already fell in love a long time ago. There's a need in me that goes deeper than the love any guy can give me; a peace that reaches past my understanding and surrounds me even tighter than his strong arms.

So maybe it isn't so ironic that I'm here walking beside this silvery sea all by myself.

I remember crying over a guy beside this same stretch of ocean. The next year, I talked to another guy on the phone while I sat on the beach, drawing hearts in the sand. I've made so many big decisions here about relationships and jobs and life in general.

Here, I walk out on the beach with my pajama pants rolled up in the morning, and I can feel the sun rise warm and orange on my face. I think about when I was a little girl and how I used to love the feeling of sunlight on my face then, too. I thought maybe God felt warm like that, and I closed my eyes and wondered what it would feel like to kiss His cheek. Was it whiskery, like my grandfather's, or airy like a cloud?

Here, I walk on the beach at night and remember walking on the beach with my dad when I was 18. My life was about to change in so many ways. I was so thankful I had my dad to hang onto. I kept throwing my head back to look at a canopy of stars above us, thinking about how God calls them by name. And He knows my name, too. I wondered if when He sings over me (as Zephaniah 3 says He does) it sounds soft and beautiful like the wind over the water or loud and unrefined like the band playing on the pier.

Here, by the water, I realize I am so in love it hurts.

Jesus isn't some spiritual boyfriend I have up in the sky; He is far more important to me than that. Even when I finally realize I've met the amazing guy I'll spend the rest of my life with, I know this much is true: I have already fallen in love with the One who waited by the well. And as I allow His perfect love to fill my life, it becomes harder and harder for me to slip on a paperdoll disguise. I want what only my God can give me: a love that is permanent, powerful and real.

Love changes perspective on a place. I could fall asleep thinking about all the other couples on the beach, or the obnoxious noise the rail makes when it clangs against the balcony, or how I wished there was a hand laced in mine when I watched the sunset tonight. But I won't do that. Instead, I'll fall asleep tonight with the window open, listening to the song caught in the wind and the water. I'll wonder if God's heartbeat thunders like that; like the ocean crashing onto the rocks. Then I'll close my eyes and imagine my head on His chest, just listening to the sound of His heart. I'll whisper a familiar prayer into the darkness: that He would be my comforter, my heart's keeper, my joy. My freefall.

Confessions

*Lord, I am trusting You to write a beautiful story
out of my longing, my rejection and my mistakes.
Write a story I never saw coming; one better
than I imagined. When I try to do this, I mess it up.
But You created this heart, and You know it completely.
I believe You know what You're doing when it comes
to my heart. I believe You are asking me to wait on
Your timing so I can experience Your best for me.
Forgive me for giving too much of my heart away.
Give me the strength I need to recommit all of me—
heart, mind, soul, and strength—to You.*

Notes

1. Shannon Ethridge, *Every Woman's Battle* (Colorado Springs: WaterBrook Press; 2003), p. 23.
2. This is typically the area the Samaritan woman is known for—her love life. In her book *God's Ideal Woman* (Downer's Grove, PA: InterVarsity Press, 1976), Dorothy Pape points out how many scholars are quick to label the Samaritan woman a harlot because of the lifestyle she is assumed to be leading. Interestingly, though, Jesus never calls her that. The only time he uses that word is in Matthew 21, when he says the publicans and the *harlots* believed John and would enter the kingdom of heaven.
3. Lauren Winner, *Real Sex* (Grand Rapids, MI: Baker Publishing, 2005), pp. 10-14.
4. C.S. Lewis, *Mere Christianity* (New York: Simon and Schuster, 1996), p. 132.
5. Madeleine L'Engle, "My Sins, I Fear, Dear Lord, Lack Glamour," in *The Ordering of Love* (Colorado Springs, CO: Waterbrook Press, 2005), p. 311.

5

Dear Veruca Salt

*Self-help is no help at all. Self-sacrifice is the way, my way,
to finding yourself, your true self. What kind of deal is it to
get everything you want but lose yourself?*
MATTHEW 16:25-26, *THE MESSAGE*

*Jesus answered, "Everyone who drinks this water will be
thirsty again, but whoever drinks the water I give him will
never thirst. Indeed, the water I give him will become in him
a spring of water welling up to eternal life."*
JOHN 4:13-14

*I want the world. I want the whole world. I want to lock it all up
in my pocket. It's my bar of chocolate. Give it to me, now.*
VERUCA SALT (FROM *WILLY WONKA
AND THE CHOCOLATE FACTORY*)

Late one night when I couldn't sleep, I grabbed a Diet Coke
(probably not wise), flopped down on my couch, and started
mindlessly flipping though the TV channels. In less than 10
minutes, I formed a hypothesis: Late night TV is not television's finest hour. For a while, I watched infomercials (those are
weirdly funny sometimes). But then I found a show with a
more intriguing concept: birthday parties. That night's episode
revolved around a guy planning his sixteenth birthday party.
I started getting nostalgic, because I remember my sixteenth
birthday party well.

I ate pizza with my family.

My dad gave me a set of golf clubs (short ones, so I could use them).

I went to the movies with my friends.

My best friend, Melanie (whose birthday was close to mine), got to drive her car to Wal-Mart for the first time. And I got to ride with her. We were so excited about our first driving venture sans parents that I'm sure people who passed us thought we were headed to the beach.

Several months later, when I had proved to my parents that the detour through my neighbor's yard in my dad's car was a one-time event, I got my first car. It was used, had air conditioning and a great radio, and rattled like a teal rocket when I went over 50. I thought it was adorable. Sixteen was a fun year.

So, I pulled my blanket tighter around my shoulders and watched someone else's sixteenth year begin. It was nothing like mine. For almost half an hour, the guy flew back and forth across the country in his private jet, trying to find the right animal to ride in for the grand entrance to his party. When the show ended, he seemed traumatized because there was no white tiger or giraffe or whatever exotic creature he had hoped to get.

The next episode wasn't much better. The girl cried—like sat down on the pavement and *sobbed*—because her parents wouldn't give her a brand new fully loaded SUV on her birthday. They wanted to give it to her the day after. By the time the show ended, I decided the infomercial on metal detectors would have been more entertaining.

Watching that weirdness was like watching paperdolls on parade. While I don't collect paperdolls, I'll admit that paperdoll art has become more interesting to me since I started comparing Sam's life to mine. I've learned that sometimes artists devote their entire trade to making paperdolls. They might create them to look like contemporary celebrities or design their clothes based on a line from an actual designer. The premise doesn't really seem to change, however: paperdoll bodies, and usually even their faces, are quite similar. What sets a paperdoll apart is what she wears.

Paperdoll books come with pages and pages of dresses and accessories ready to be cut out and tabbed against the doll's body: a high-priced bag, a pair of red heels, a short black dress, even a little furry dog. At first, she may look just like any other paperdoll—big smile, hair with a delicate curl. But the accessories set her apart. You look at what she has and get a good feeling for what she is about, which is fine, because she's paper.

But people aren't supposed to be that easy to read. People aren't supposed to be two-dimensional.

The more I read the conversation that Jesus had with the Samaritan woman and thought about what that conversation might look like against my heart and my status-obsessed world, I could see a sad paperdoll similarity: I try to make life an accessory as well.

Sam has already shown me plenty of other ways to be paper. Sometimes my paper smile disguises sin, loneliness and shame. Sometimes I've given all my love and energy to making myself into a woman who will be loved and valued because she's beautiful. Sometimes I've become a paperdoll by trying to become this whole other version of a girl I want some guy to love.

Jesus knows we struggle in all those areas, and by the well He offered Sam a real alternative to the love that kept leaving her empty: living water.

This gift applies just as much to an obsession with stuff. Sometimes I go paperdoll when it comes to thinking that real life can be worn or bought—that it can be tabbed over my shoulders and arms. I live in a world that places a high priority and importance on what I wear, own and have, and I feed into that goal with all my heart, all my mind, all my soul and all my strength. Materialism is a deadly and dangerous paradigm for living.

All that talk about pricey cars and white tigers made me wonder how anybody could be so shallow. Who really lives life like that? Who seriously believes that kind of life is important?

The answer was wired immediately from my brain to my heart: I do.

Of course, my birthday parties usually involve board games and homemade cupcakes, not strobe lights and limos. I may not care about what kind of car I drive (though I like to think the coffee stains all over the floorboards give it character), and I could care less what car my friends drive. But I can think of plenty of times I've approached life with an ungrateful spirit. I've seen something I thought I had to have to make my life feel full. Sometimes it's a bag or clothes or a cell phone. Other times it's a relationship, a different job, or losing just 10 more pounds. Like a brainless paperdoll, I make mental lists of the accessories, achievements and awards I need to have attached to my body and my life for wholeness to ensue.

When I'm operating with that mentality, nothing satisfies.

There was only one word that seemed to be a rally cry for both teens on this show: *more*. The whole motivating factor for these uber-wealthy 16-year-olds was to have the biggest and best party their town had ever seen. Money was no object. They wanted a nicer party than their friends had, a celebrity cake cutter their friends couldn't afford, and a car their friends would never be able to drive.

What they owned, and wore, seemed to define them completely. But beneath the paper exterior seemed to be a much deeper longing. Erwin McManus sheds some brilliant light on what that longing really is in his book *Soul Cravings*:

> I don't think its incidental that over the past twenty years the labels on our clothes moved from the inside to the outside. We know who we are by our symbols and we can identify those who belong to our tribe by reading the signs. Izod has an alligator, Polo has a rider, A&F has a moose, Lucky Brand has a shamrock . . . something as meaningless as moving the labels to the outside could actually have deeper spiritual implica-

tions. Is it possible that we are all created with a need to belong to something, to belong to someone, and the less we actually belong to each other, the more symbols we need to feel like we belong to each other?[1]

Our obsession with stuff is about a much deeper need than we realize. When we think belonging can be branded or that life is a product, we're bound for a trip to the well. Materialism hampers our spiritual maturity, deadlocks our ability to live an intentional life and, perhaps most tragically, blinds us to the needs of a dying world.

Our obsession with stuff is a deep well, one where we drink up every drop of "life" and still feel thirsty.

Forever Sixteen

I don't think an obsession with stuff is just a problem for jet-setting 16-year-olds on TV. If we aren't careful, an obsession with stuff and status will plague us all the way from 16 to 96. The compulsion we had as a teen for the most expensive jeans and the best new cell phone can mold into an obsession as an adult with having a better car and nicer pool than the neighbors. There are unsatisfied 17-year-olds, maxing out credit cards as they try to find love in a lifestyle of extravagance. And there are unsatisfied 27-year-olds, trying really hard to convince people they're cool, and edgy, and worth loving. And maxing out credit cards as they try to find love through what they own.

Advertising feeds into this compulsion. Between driving to school and work, getting online, looking through magazines and newspapers and watching TV, you're exposed to hundreds of different ads a day. A lot of money and creativity has been put into making that ad a sensory experience for you. Think about the billboards you see when you drive, which are designed to catch your imagination and get stuck in your mind. Magazine and television ads are never just about a product; they are about a lifestyle. Even my email is revolting against me. I get news feeds on the side bar, advertising products my email company knows women my age might be interested in. I haven't lost the irony of living in a consumer society. Some days, I feel consumed by ad campaigns designed to make me feel incomplete and lacking.

Those paperdolls whisper a tempting secret: *my worth is based on what I own.*

And it isn't just this culture that struggles with a keen obsession for stuff. I just read a story in *National Geographic* about a mummified lion discovered in an Egyptian tomb. The author pointed out how lions were revered in Egypt, worshiped as gods and, in this situation, given a burial reserved for only the important and influential. The Egyptians held to a belief that they could take their treasures—everything from their jewelry to their pets—with them into the afterlife. They thought that as long as these things were buried with them, they would make it past this world and into the next. They wanted to make sure the afterlife was cloaked in the same riches as the life they had led on earth.

Here's the reality: their stuff is still there, crumbling into a big dust pile. The lion is still in the tomb, only now it's literally a bag of bones. I love history and appreciate the significance of historic relics, but there's a point to be made here about wealth and possessions: the people are gone; their stuff is still there. They didn't take anything with them at all. At the end of the day, whether you buy it in a gift shop, a junk store or a tomb sale, possessions still crumble.

In the end, wealth doesn't seem to matter much.

History yields another example, one that might ring all too clearly in our paperdoll moments. King Solomon was one of the wealthiest men in the world. He had palaces, money, wives and the best of everything brought to him. There was nothing available in his culture that his money and status couldn't have afforded him. But his overwhelming theme in Ecclesiastes is simply this: "Everything is meaningless" (1:2).

Picture King Solomon writing late into the night, scrawling out sentences about his life, his possessions and his worth. Picture the candlelight flickering off the ornate table tops, high ceilings and treasured relics of his palace. Picture him surrounded by everything his world could offer.

"Meaningless," he calls it. It's a cry echoed throughout history and through our modern world.

"Without love," says Paul in his first letter to the Corinthians, "I am nothing" (see 1 Cor. 13:2).

And love cannot be packaged and sold.

There by the well, Sam was about to discover something crucial: she had an important message to carry. We have an important message to carry to the world as well, and I'm learning that much of that message depends on whether I will choose to impact my culture with love or let my culture consume me.

I'm nobody's paperdoll. I want a love that lends itself to wholeness and fullness, not a love that crumbles away like pottery shards in a tomb.

Secrets and Sparrows

When I'm on a long road trip, I begin to realize that my society is having a huge impact on me. Inevitably, if I've been in my car for longer than half an hour, I start to crave coffee. I drum my fingers against the steering wheel. My eyes scan signs, billboards and distant horizons for the little green circle that will bring me so much joy. When I find it, celebration ensues. Before I even see the letters, I know the green mermaid symbol. I exit and nab a double mocha for the road, quest complete.

In fact, when I think about it, my life is centered around brands. When I'm in a new mall, I keep my eyes open for a bright white apple. I know the design on the back pocket of my favorite jeans, and I can instantly find them in a sea of denim.

I know my favorite stores, book series and, sometimes, even bands by their logo. I'll bet you do too.

So try this: picture yourself staring at a wall in an art museum. On that wall are emblems, logos and brands from the stores, companies and products that define Western culture. You may use those brands, or you may not, but the point is that they are very prominent in the world you live in. They represent a culture with unlimited resources. And, sometimes, when obsession takes over, they represent a fast track to faux happiness.

Now picture the silhouette of a brown bird projected against that same wall.

When Jesus was talking to His disciples and describing how beloved they were, He used the image of a sparrow to convey His tender concern. This is what He said:

> Are not two sparrows sold for a penny? Yet not one of them will fall to the ground apart from the will of your Father. And even the very hairs of your head are all numbered. So don't be afraid; you are worth more than many sparrows (Matt. 10:29-31).

Of all the birds in creation, sparrows are probably one of the least notable. They are small, fragile and fairly common. But God's eye is on the most fragile creatures. If He notices when a sparrow breaks a wing, then He of course notices us. He's keyed into the details of our hearts, offering us real and true love. Just like in Samaria, He's looking past even our questions to see into the deepest needs of our hearts—needs that no amount of "stuff" can satisfy. Our discontent doesn't go unnoticed, but He wants to fill it with something deeper. He wants us to fill up on life; on real life.

There by the well in Samaria, Jesus offered Sam a key to abundant life: living water. This is water that doesn't get old or stale. It never becomes irrelevant. It is constant and deep enough to reach into the most desperate cry of longing in our hearts. And it cannot be bought. When we experience living water, we can also experience something that seems to be so illusive: contentment.

As I learn how to become the kind of woman who impacts a culture with love without becoming a greedy paperdoll, I find myself praying for strength in a few areas.

I Want to Live in Moderation and Keep Eternal Perspective

I don't think buying a new pair of jeans hampers my intimacy with God. But I think there's a dangerous pattern in my paperdoll culture when clothes, cars and money become synonymous with belonging. In Matthew 6:28, Jesus uses nature to remind us that our worth isn't bound together by a thread. "And why do you worry about clothes?" He asks. "See how the lilies of the field grow. They do not labor or spin."

The issue seems to be about not only living within my means but also living under my means and walking constantly in the light of His love. Love is the issue at hand. Am I buying things I can afford, or am I maxing out my credit cards to fill up a void that only God can fill? Our stuff will, eventually, end up in a dirt pile (whether that is in a tomb or a junk store). But love is something that lasts.

> Do not store up for yourselves treasures on earth, where moth and rust destroy, and where thieves break in and steal. But store up for yourselves treasures in heaven, where moth and rust do not destroy, and where thieves do not break in and steal. For where your treasure is, there your heart will be also (Matt. 6:19-21).

Love is permanent and eternal. Stuff is not. When we are living in the fullness of God—living the colorful, exciting, bright, confusing life He called us to live—we can look at everything our world offers, every shiny gift, and know when to say "enough." And in a world of excess, learning to say enough is liberating.

"When you wake up in the morning or spend your day free from needing to run to the mall or look online and buy all this stuff, you're going to have a freedom in your spirit that's going to be a great way to live." — Nancy Ortberg[2]

I Want to Live Out "the Secret"

Advertisers think they know a secret about us: we will buy anything if we think it will help us to become more loved. They make perfume and clothing ads look all dreamy and gorgeous, all avant-garde and enticing. The girl wearing the clothes we want looks happy and beautiful . . . and she's locked in the arms of a beautiful guy. They want us to associate the product with her lifestyle (which may not be her lifestyle at all) and think that if we just had *that*, then we would be as confident and elegant as she is. They try to convince us that the secret to *being* more beautiful, more happy and more content is *having* more.

But Paul tells us a different secret in the book of Philippians. And this secret has the potential to make our paper hearts soar:

> I know what it is to be in need, and I know what it is to
> have plenty. I have learned the secret of being content
> in any and every situation, whether well fed or hungry,
> whether living in plenty or in want (Phil. 4:12).

Paul wasn't writing words about contentment from a posh suite overlooking the park. These particular words were written from a dark prison cell. He sincerely lived the life he wrote about. In every situation, Paul drew on Christ's strength, and he did something else: he gave thanks (see 1 Thess. 5:18).

In my own life, I'm prone to complaining when life is actually not that bad. But if Paul is right, and if I learn to live in gratitude, the way I look at my life and what I own might drastically change. It might change me, and it might change the world.

I decided to put this thought into practice. One year while traveling to Georgia for Turkeypalooza (i.e., Thanksgiving) with my family, our car began moving at a sluggish pace through Atlanta traffic. Then, as is common, the car came to a complete stop. I instinctively jerked my headphones off to start complaining, but I was quickly silenced. Out my window was the Atlanta skyline, sparkling fiercely into the black night. I had gotten so involved in the traffic jam in front of me that I had forgotten about the city surrounding me.

I pulled my journal out of my bag and started writing down what I was thankful for at that particular point in my life (it seemed appropriate for the season). This is what I came up with:

I'm thankful for blue-sky Sundays, rainy days when I can sleep in, stars all over the sky, first snowfalls and endless rows of gray mountains. I'm thankful for city skylines, for friends who love me and look out for me in a giant new place. I'm thankful for amazing parents, who let me test my wings when I get wild new ideas—despite inevitable ulcers. I'm thankful for strong hugs goodnight, and sad hugs goodbye. I'm thankful for that little spark of affection that comes when I least expect it, for the sweet guys who tell me I look cute even when I look like a total trash heap. I'm thankful for a job that doesn't pay much but allows me time to pursue what I love. I'm thankful for nights I write so much I see the first glimpse of sunrise. I'm thankful for music—endless, amazing, wonderful music to match every mood.

I'm thankful for my brother and my sister, who are both such amazing people and friends. I'm thankful for my niece. Two years ago she asked me to do arts and crafts, and now she wants advice on an outfit that is "trendy but not too trendy, like burger-joint trendy." I'm thankful for Andy [my nephew] and the education I have been given on Thomas the Train at his disposal. I'm thankful for tomorrow; the one day, in a whole

year of days, when I can anticipate candlelight and conversa-
tion and lots of face time with the people I love most.

   I'm thankful for cell phones and emails, for calls and notes
and mixed CDs even when life gets busy. I'm thankful for
plays, for my car (seven years and still going strong!), the way
my treadmill sounds when it's at that 2.9 whir. I'm thankful
for my scars and freckles, two things I used to despise but have
actually come to love. I'm thankful for great novels, good movies
and beautiful poetry. I'm thankful for mall trips with Melanie,
old home movies, contact lenses and glasses with dark frames.
I'm thankful for people who make me laugh.

   I'm thankful for the Word I keep falling more and more in
love with, for the intimate moments of prayer that center my
day, and for the opportunity to see new places, meet new peo-
ple, write, and learn and live in a place where I can talk about
what's on my mind and in my heart. And I'm thankful for
memories and moments that hurt a little at first. I'm thankful
for every card my papaw sent me on my birthday, for every
Saturday I spent at his house, for every song we sang while he
played his guitar. His Bible is sitting on my shelf at home, taped
together around the edges. Sometimes I read it and imagine
hearing his voice. I think of the memories I had with him, and
the ones I will have, and how God's story keeps tying all the
ends of my life together. I'm thankful for my now and for my
eternity. Thank You, God, for this beautiful messy life . . .

The list went on and on and on. By the end of it, I could feel
tears stinging my eyes. My life was pretty confusing at that
point. There were plenty of unanswered questions. My grandfather had just passed away, and my family was still grieving the
loss. But I could see how God had blessed me and loved me
through all the unknowns. When I sat down and started trying
to list everything I was thankful for, uncertainty gave way to
peace. Gratitude isn't just for modern-day Pollyannas who go
around singing about sunshine and rainbows. Gratitude is for

girls who, sometimes, get caught in the shadows for a while. Thankfulness is essential in those moments, too.

That night, stuck in traffic, watching the Atlanta skyline flicker out the window, I was overwhelmed with the kindness of God, who knows my every need, who sees my deepest desire, who picks up fragile little sparrows and helps them fly again.

Show Me How I Can Give in Love Until I'm Spent

I know most of us aren't at a place right now where we're rolling in financial resources. But we aren't too young to realize that every resource we have—be it money, or creativity, or education—belongs to God. We aren't given money and gifts and dreams just for our own comfort and enjoyment. We are meant to share them with the world.

Learning to channel our education, our resources and our passions into legit causes can be one of the most exciting adventures we will ever experience. Giving counters materialism in a wild way. My friends have given me some pretty fabulous examples of cheerful giving:

- While we were at a youth conference, my friends Caitlyn, Erica and Michelle heard a speaker talk about Compassion International. For 30 bucks a month, one child would be able to go to school, eat healthy food, get medical care and be discipled. The girls were all moved to do something . . . but they didn't know what. They were just starting college at the time and, like most college students, 30 bucks a month was steep. However, they realized that together, they would only be out 10 bucks a month. That was doable. So every month, they put in 10 dollars each to sponsor a little guy in South America. The girls are giving what they have, and the payback they receive (pictures of him smiling, school reports, letters about his progress) is bigger than any payday you can imagine.

• No holiday screams Consumerfest like Christmas. The season that should remind us of Jesus' birth and family traditions can backfire fast. The crowds, background music and color give the malls a bizarre carnival atmosphere at that time of year. Suddenly, you remember your great aunt's cousin's sister's best friend and how much she would like the salt and pepper shakers that look like corgis. One of the best ways I use my resources at Christmas, and keep my heart where it needs to be, is by filling up a shoebox with toys and sending it to a little boy or girl via Samaritan's Purse. The whole project can cost less than 20 dollars, and it feels much better than buying junk my friends will just return anyway. My friend Sarah and I also have a cool Christmas tradition. Instead of buying something for each other, we pick a name off the angel tree, go shop for that girl's list, and then we go eat together.

• Jimmy, a friend and talented Brooklyn based artist, volunteered his time to do some art projects with the kids in his church. The paintings they created were then sold in the church's coffee shop, and the money all went to Heifer International, a humanitarian aid program.

There are plenty of ways that we can become better givers; the key issue is giving in love. So if you're blessed with money, be it now or in the future, give as much as you can. And if you're blessed with other resources—like time, creativity or energy—give those things away in love.

Somehow, giving has a way of becoming as much a gift for the giver as the recipient. Contentment rains down over our hearts the moment we choose to put love into action. And giving in love sends a beautiful message to a broken world.

What Will Your Message Be?

I remember the first time I set foot in a third-world country. What I'd only seen in commercials was suddenly in vibrant 3-D. Human waste pooled in the streets. Houses made of boards and plywood dotted the hills. Scrawny dogs trotted around, their rib bones protruding from their skin. It seemed like everything that was so iconic about the American Dream—the house, the dog, the white picket fence—was twisted around and given new meaning in this place.

But the picture I'll never forget is when I walked into a school there in the slums. The kids at that Compassion site were receiving education, food, medical care, clothing and discipleship. It was just like the scene in *The Wizard of Oz* when Dorothy steps from black and white into color. The world in the walls of that school was so alive with joy.

I remember thinking of how sweet it was that these kids will grow up associating the image of Jesus Christ with caring for the poor and hurting. They won't associate the name of Jesus with flashy things, such as money, nice cars, flat screens or fancy phones. The adorable kids at the Compassion site will always associate the name of Jesus with being fed, loved, held and cared for. They won't think of Christians as careless and standoffish or as people who repeat eloquent clichés with no action. Instead, they will see what the Body of Christ can really look like. They will be able to point to a specific place in their life when their deepest needs—physical and spiritual—were met. They have living water. In a land of muted colors, mud and poverty, life is still abundant.

I remember sitting in the back of one small classroom, feeling the sweat dripping off my forehead and trying to swallow down the lump in my throat. As a group of little kids sang Spanish songs about Jesus, His name rising up out of the slums like a symphony, I wondered what message I would carry to the world.

My country is carrying a message to the world. Sometimes it's a good message: we will work to feed the hungry, clothe the naked and find medical help for those who desperately need it and can't afford it. But sometimes the message is hidden in the face of a paperdoll: love can be bought. It is a car. A perfume. A diamond-crusted version of life those people will never know. The message of materialism will reach the world.

But we have been given a more powerful, more wonderful message to carry: the message of hope and love found in Christ.

Discontent and materialism blind us to a dying world. Our enemy wants us to become so self-absorbed that we can't look past our mirror. He wants us to trade off intimacy with God for unsatisfying pursuits. He wants us to become so obsessed with having better cars and parties and celebrity cake cutters that we won't spend our time doing what matters. He wants us to think living life to the fullest means stockpiling more future antiques.

There is a dangerous mentality that creeps into our subconscious on paperdoll days. It goes something like this: "You're young and you have all the time in the world, so just enjoy life." It is true that you may be young, but you have no idea how much time you actually have. So fill that time with real life. Use that time to carry a message that changes hearts and lives.

Let love define you, not another label.

Dearest Veruca

Have you ever seen the movie *Willy Wonka and the Chocolate Factory* (the old one with Gene Wilder)? This movie pays homage to a girl whom I believe to be one of literature's most quirky and intriguing brats. Roald Dahl wrote the character of Veruca Salt to mirror the sin of greed. The movie, though it changes some aspects of her story, portrays her perfectly. Her tantrums are obnoxious and comical (and weirdly similar to the tantrums those 15-year-olds threw over their birthday parties). Veruca has no qualms about getting everything she wants, regardless of what it costs or who it might inconvenience. She wants *more*. She is never happy with what she owns. She is convinced that more stuff will satisfy her longing.

Her swan song in the movie comes when she sees a room of geese that lay golden eggs. Veruca is enamored at the sight. She loses any semblance of reasoning, believing the golden egg will be everything she wants and more, and demands that her father procure a goose for her. As is often true of such pursuits, things do not end well for Veruca.

In looking through all these issues of greed, materialism, obsession and living water—and what that really looks like in a life—I decided that Veruca and I probably had a few things in common. And so, this would be my letter to her:

Dear Veruca:

Your grand finale song in Wonka Tower has always been a personal favorite of mine, and I think I have finally discovered why. For years, I've convinced myself that we are very different, you and me. I decided I wasn't as selfish as you (or as obnoxious), but I also decided that I would never scream over the silly things you seem to be obsessed with, like golden tickets or golden eggs. What is it with you and gold?

Lately, though, I've been rethinking this issue. I've tried to fill my life up with silly things, too. I am guilty of wanting all the wrong things—golden eggs that scramble into big golden breakfasts and then are gone. (I would abandon that dream if I were you. Next year, the oompa loompas will probably build a more durable egg anyway, one that fits in your pocket and has Internet access.)

I scream as loud as you because I am surrounded and inundated by the pressure to have more stuff. I think I'll taste life more fully when I have it, but sometimes what seems sweet goes sour in my mouth. I'm beginning to see that golden eggs are all too common in my world, but that contentment is not. This is some dangerous ground you're dancing on, V.

Take a look at all your greedy little friends. They're getting stuck in chocolate shoots and turning into blueberries and burping bubbles the size of baseballs. You are no different than them. You want something all the candy in the world won't satisfy. You keep screaming. You keep getting what you want. But what you want, or get, isn't making you happy.

I think I know why.

For me, it sometimes takes sitting on a rotten egg pile to realize my heart's most piercing cry: I want love. I want something real. I'm tired of sugary imitations. I'm tired of buying the right clothes and driving the right car just to prove I matter.

It's all eggshells and pottery shards in the end. The stuff you want is just stuff. A year from now, you probably won't even remember you wanted it. One hundred years from now, you'll be gone, and the stuff will be dirt.

Before you dust rotten eggshells off your designer dress, think about this: you have the potential to leave behind something good and real. You can experience a love that matters and moves you.

"Taste and see that the LORD is good," is what the Psalmist writes (see Ps. 34:8). That kind of love will root deep into your soul, flood your senses, change the way you see the world.

Golden eggs, golden tickets and 10,000 tons of ice cream will never satisfy your deepest longing. Or mine. But this love, this one perfect love, will.

You know what's kind of ironic? Gold doesn't matter much to Him. Gold is just pavement up there. You can put on your Asics and run on the stuff. His goodness doesn't shower down in gold coins and gold tickets. I see it in compassion, in passionate advocacy, in imagination, in His creation and in His people. He offers a secret to survive all the fake—genuine gratitude. He offers a treasure too beautiful to be paired with a jingle—love that never crumbles or goes away.

I've decided that is what I really want. Because when I'm living in the fullness of His love—when I'm loving His people, when I'm walking through this world looking for how I can give, when I'm watching the sun sink down into the mountains, glittering, glowing, reflecting His glory for me to see—it's that moment, loved by God and sharing His love, that I feel like the richest girl in the world.

His love will blow your mind. Taste and see.

Love (and golden eggshells),
Me

Confessions

*Lord, teach me to use the resources I have
to make a difference that will last. When I have
money to give, show me where to give it. When I don't
even have that, show me where I can give my heart,
my creativity and my education for Your glory.
I'm guilty of feeding into this lie that more stuff
will make me happy, but I know that only You
define my worth. What I really want is more of You.
I want Your love to be my only label.*

Notes

1. Erwin McManus, *Soul Cravings* (Nashville, TN: Thomas Nelson, 2006), entry 15.
2. Nancy Ortberg, "Burning Issues," *Relevant Magazine*, May/June 2008.

Some Place Sudden, Dark and Deep

*"Sir," the woman said, "you have nothing to draw with and
the well is deep. Where can I get this living water?"*
JOHN 4:11

*And what was said to the rose to make it unfold was said to me,
here in my chest. So be quiet now, and rest.*
DAVID CROWDER

*If a heart breaking made a sound, I wonder what it would be:
a blanket falling on grass, water freezing, a door closing
or a silent scream. This night feels like it will last forever.
But I'm holding out for the promise of sunrise.
It will reach its arms in defiance across the dark night . . .
quiet, pink and bright. It will sound like a new
beginning. It will color every corner of the night with
new beginnings. Light will reach into every dark corner soon.
And then I know life prevails. And love lasts forever.
So through these tears I watch the stars come out, one by one.
I hold my heart out to the only One who can make it whole.
And I wait for sunrise.*

I'm learning that beauty can hide in some of the most unexpected places and circumstances. An ordinary slice of life freezes
like a still shot in my mind and I know I'll never forget it. Like
trees full of green apples with a blue sky in the background.

Creamer when it swirls into black coffee. Light blue eggs in a bird's nest. Orange leaves on the black pavement in October. The shadow of the maple tree on the wall in my old bedroom. Footprints dissolving in sand. Texas sunsets. Stars canopied above the mountains. The London Tower Bridge at night.

But more than heart shots of places, I remember these random mental snapshots of people I love.

I remember my dad holding my nephew Andy on the beach one summer night, pointing toward the horizon at the lights on the fishing boats. The lights blinked like magic against the dark water. I remember Thanksgiving at my sister's house last year and the way candlelight bent through tall glasses and sparkled against the cranberry walls. The eight very different laughs that rose in unison from the table were the only music I could hear and the only music that could have truly captured the moment. I think of my mom clipping pink roses and tossing seeds in the soft garden ground. I think of my family crowded into my grandparents' house at Christmas. I remember the drawl in all our accents, the sound of the coffeemaker sputtering, and how good it felt to hug people I never get to see. I remember welcome-home hugs at airports, Krispy Kreme runs in my pajamas with my roommates in college, and standing arm in arm singing "Hey Jude" with my friends (and a million British people) in Hyde Park.

Sometimes, beautiful seizes my heart when I see a wedding kiss or a snowball fight or feel a strong hand reach over to hold mine. It happens when I'm having dinner with my best friends, riding in a convertible with my sister, or praying in a circle of exhausted teenagers about to board a church bus home. When I hear someone play guitar, I remember Chase playing guitar with my grandfather. I could be wearing a gorgeous black dress, sitting in an Italian opera, and the experience still wouldn't compare to sitting in my grandfather's carport listening to him play songs on his guitar. Love is the sonnet, the symphony and the rock opera that truly moves me.

So many ordinary days, and memories, thread through my life like that. They break my heart and make me feel simultaneously awestruck and incredibly grateful. I think maybe the most beautiful things in the world—the ones that get caught in my mind—have something in common: love.

There is another picture of love that still takes my breath away when I think about it. I know I will never forget it. And it didn't happen at a spring afternoon or at a wedding. It happened at a funeral.

Goodbye for Now

I walked in one of the back doors of the church that day, doing my best to avert my eyes from the casket at the front of the room. Funerals are always awkward and sad, but this one was, by far, the most surreal I had ever attended. I tried to keep my eyes glued to the plush pink carpet, but movement near the front of the auditorium stopped me. I looked up, stopped moving and felt a tear slide down my face. In the front of the room, I saw Katie's hospital bed, rolled in beside Paxton's casket, because she wanted to say goodbye.

Katie and Paxton were destined to be best friends. They were first cousins who grew up in the same town and went to the same school, and they were mostly a package deal. Wherever one of them was, the other was nearby. They finished each other's sentences and argued like sisters. They had more in common than a genetic code. Gorgeous blondes with infectious laughs, they were both natural leaders. Just a few months earlier, both girls had committed their lives to Christ at the same church service. I could see, immediately, how their decision had permeated their lives. Their love for God was a sincere passion and it poured out in genuine, beautiful ways around their classmates and friends. They were destined to do life together, to tackle all the big questions, pray each other through the hard times, and keep each other accountable.

Then everything changed.

On an ordinary day after an ordinary outing, their car crashed. Katie's injuries were severe and life-changing. And Paxton immediately went home to be with the Lord.

In the days following the accident, when life was at an awkward pause for everyone involved, I took out our pictures from a girls' trip. Not even a year previous, we'd all been hanging out in a hotel together, ordering pizza at midnight, praying together and worshiping God with hundreds of other girls in a church. I looked at my pics of the two of them: making funny faces with French fries coming out of their mouths like walrus teeth . . . huddled together with other girls in one of those pictures where half the group is smiling and half the group is making a goofy face . . . hanging out in the hotel, just laughing, with beautiful smiles that looked so similar.

They were meant to do life together. They were meant to help each other get ready for the prom. They were meant to help each other pack for college, be bridesmaids in each other's weddings, and have kids that grew up and became best friends as well. These girls were intentional about their living abundant lives. And now one was moving on without the other one.

New heart pictures began to file in behind the old ones. Now I could see a table filled with flowers, stuffed animals that Paxton's friends brought, baby pictures, homecoming pictures, sports paraphernalia and orange balloons (which fit, somehow—something oddly bright in all the sadness). I watched Paxton's mom comfort teammates and friends of her daughter with a tender mix of grief and grace. Katie also came to the funeral too. She couldn't walk because of her injuries and had to come in her hospital bed. Her mouth was wired shut, and scars zigzagged up her arm.

Standing in the back of the room, watching the scene unfold, only one thought wove through my mind: *Katie will never survive this.*

Death makes no sense when you're 100, much less when you're 16. And this wasn't just an acquaintance who had died; this was her best friend. It was as if part of her heart had died. I knew that she would physically survive. She would do therapy and learn to walk again. The physical scars would fade. She would go back to school eventually, drive again, date and go to college. But much deeper than the physical was a girl who was incredibly brokenhearted. How do you function when part of your heart has been ripped away like that? I couldn't wrap my brain around one iota of what was happening. So I didn't try. I could only watch Katie reach one scarred arm over to touch her best friend's hand.

The paramedics finally wheeled Katie's bed back and collapsed it center aisle beside her mom. Guitars started to thump, and hundreds of voices lifted up a praise chorus. "Blessed be the name of the Lord," they sang.

You give and take away, but my heart will choose to say, "Lord, blessed be Your name."

The words became a prayer, a rally cry and a source of hope for a grieving family. They were confused and hurt, but they held onto a specific promise. They weren't left alone in the deep.

The Deepest Well

In the theater of your mind, focus back in on the exchange between Jesus and Sam by the well. She's come upon this Jewish man asking her for a drink, which is weird in itself. And then He takes it a step further . . . He offers her living water. She makes what seems like a very natural, and rather obvious, observation: "Sir . . . you have nothing to draw with and the well is deep" (John 4:11).

The well the Samaritan woman stood by was, literally, a deep well. Archaeologists believe they've discovered the site of Jacob's Well there in Samaria, and over the years they've made plenty of guestimations on how far into the ground it goes. The exact depth isn't known, but when the site was cleaned out in 1935, it was found to be 138 feet deep.[1] That's more than 10 stories. No wonder drawing water from the thing was such a chore. And remember, this was the only water source for miles and miles. Jesus' offer to give Sam water with no bucket seemed absurd.

But Jesus, of course, was talking about a different kind of water.

Living water isn't made of two parts hydrogen and one part oxygen. Jesus was offering her eternal life and—this is key—life abundant there by the well. He was offering permanent, unconditional love; something that filled up empty places. He was offering her living water that would satisfy her soul and her deepest needs.

He was offering her a love that heals. Jesus, who walked the earth as fully God and fully man, was able to look beyond the physical, beyond the paperdoll smile, and see her real need.

When Sam said, "the well is deep," she could just as easily have been talking about the pain in her own heart. She wasn't just packing along heavy water jars to the well that day; she was also carrying the weight that comes from life's most unpredictable circumstances. She was alone. She probably knew rejection. She had experienced grief, and whether it came from someone leaving her, divorcing her or someone dying, the point is that she'd experienced loss five times over. She was currently in the arms of another man, but that wasn't helping, either.

The lives we lead, inevitably, come with seasons of incredible pain. The unexpected heartaches, the words people say, the things people do and the decisions we make ourselves leave deep scars that we don't expect anyone to really understand. We try to smile brave, paper smiles until our faces hurt, but our hearts carry deep emotional wounds.

Maybe that is one of the greatest lessons we can learn by the well. Someone sees our deepest places of pain. They don't go unnoticed, and they don't go unattended. Our deepest places of shame, regret, loss, sorrow and tragedy tend to affect us so deeply that we think no one can offer hope.

But He is not like anyone else we've ever met.

Behind My Paper Smile

We've talked about what it means to be a modern-day paper-doll and parade around with the right labels and right stuff because we believe that what we own makes us matter. Or how we can become paper by trying to make ourselves into the girl we think some guy will fall in love with. We see other women and do our best to mold our heart and life to their life, thinking love only comes from an unreachable standard of external beauty.

But there's another kind of paperdoll I'm guilty of becoming—a whole other kind of fake I slip on and off as easily as a cheap Halloween costume—and that's pretending I'm "fine" when my heart feels ripped to pieces. I convince myself that God doesn't care about my deepest places of hurt. I'm afraid to tell anybody how I feel, because (1) they won't get it, and (2) they'll just think I'm complaining.

A paperdoll isn't just a metaphor for an infatuation with externals; it's a tragic metaphor for a girl who looks fine but who is going to pieces deep down in her heart. Even churches have a way of becoming veritable theaters where we hide our true heart, or deep pain, behind a bright mask of "fine."

Sometimes there is a tremendous amount of turmoil churning behind that paper smile. Like when we lose the people we love. Grief feels like an anchor pulling our hearts further down in our chest. It becomes hard for us to get up in the morning or go outside or think even weeks (or hours) ahead. I don't think it is ever fully possible to prepare for the emotional and physical response that grief can bring into a life.

Maybe we're facing chaos in our family. A grandparent is diagnosed with Alzheimer's. A sibling battles a life-threatening illness. We watch our families struggle under financial pressure. We move to a town where we know absolutely no one. A friend of mine was talking about her parents' divorce recently, an event that transpired when she was very young. Although both parents today are an active part of her life and both of them are walking with God, she said the scar left over is still a deep one. She remembers very little about the actual divorce, but she can still remember crying the day she found out. It's amazing how tragic memories can often be the most vivid.

We may also try to hide behind our paper smile when we feel the chains of addiction and obsession slowly tighten around us. What starts as a desire to get in shape spirals out of control. What starts as a mindless game becomes our only focus from the time we get home until we sleep at night. We wonder how in the world these things became our gods. We long for freedom. But we feel enslaved.

Being a victim of abuse can produce an incredible amount of turmoil in our lives. Even after the physical scars heal, the emotional scars still ache.

Even a moment in our past when someone has broken our hearts can have a lasting effect. So many of us have painful stories of being made fun of—whether it's because we're too tall, or overweight, or too short, or because we have a lisp, or because of our family. Words are sharper than a double-edged sword, and the scar they leave behind never really seems to fade.

The list of deep places goes on and on and on. We become beautiful paperdolls with frayed hearts, masking our pain from the world with another smile. In those moments, I even decide that if I pretend long enough, I'll start to find some semblance of inner peace. But that peace never comes from pretending. It only comes from the One who waited by the well.

We get to bring the whole entire mess of our heart to Jesus, just as it is. We get to sort out the pieces there in His presence. We get to take comfort in His love. His offer to us is the same as His offer to Sam: living water. The kind that loves us unconditionally and covers every need.

Yes, there are some deep places of pain in our hearts. But His love is deep enough to penetrate every last part.

The One Who Never Sleeps

In the months following Katie's loss, I began to see a whole new understanding of just how Jesus ministers to us in the deep places. For one, Katie is nobody's paperdoll. Grief brought with it a flood of emotions. She was hurt and angry one minute and at peace the next. Some nights she wanted to be surrounded by her friends; other nights she wanted to be alone. She could have hidden that emotion and frustration behind a paper smile, but she didn't. She never went paper. She kept drawing closer to God, even with her questions. That was one of the most incredible lessons I learned from seeing her engage life again.

God Gives Us the Freedom to Be Real

Even in our grieving, God gives us the freedom to be real before His throne. Jesus wasted no time getting to Sam's real need. I like knowing I can be genuine and real when I'm talking to Him, too. I think it is very interesting that Jesus chose to experience emotion when he walked on earth. He didn't detach from His feelings. He cried when His friend Lazarus died (even though He knew where He really was). He loved and celebrated and got angry and went through the most excruciating stress and heartbreak that anyone will ever experience.

Questioning God's timing when life goes haywire isn't a sign of spiritual immaturity. Just the fact that you are still going to God, still running to Him with your questions, shows a genuine desire for intimacy. And even when we don't get the answers we're looking for, we can know, just like Sam, that Jesus ministers to our deepest need.

He Understands What a Deep Place Feels Like

My grandmother passed away a month before Christmas. As her funeral procession made its slow drive down the center of my hometown, I looked out the window of my parents' car and cringed. Christmas decorations were everywhere. Every house and evergreen and mailbox and van (seriously—even an old van that passed us) seemed to be covered with colored lights. The electric poles down the center of my hometown were adorned with blinking snowflakes. Even billboards shouted Christmas greetings from local stores. I forgot Christmas was coming. It had never felt so dreary and sad to me before. Suddenly, a season I loved seemed to be mocking my heartache. I watched all the blinking lights blur through my tears like smeared rainbows in the December rain.

Then I remembered the real point of Christmas. I thought about how Jesus didn't come to a world that was whole but one that was dark and broken. It was a weary world that rejoiced at His coming, a world ravaged by death and destruction and loss. A world aching for a miracle from God. And from a starry night in a manger to the last shattered breath on the cross to a hollow tomb on a sunrise morning, He completed what He came to do. He came to give us eternal life; life abundant. He came so we would know we are never alone. He came to be our Prince of Peace, especially in our moments of grief.

> I have told you these things, so that in me you may have peace. In this world you will have trouble. But take heart! I have overcome the world (John 16:33).

When it comes to places of pain and loneliness, Jesus is familiar with our suffering. Jesus' entire crucifixion was unbearably painful and lonely. One of His best friends betrayed him. His other friends walked away from Him (John was the only disciple at Jesus' crucifixion). The people who had celebrated His entrance into the city of Jerusalem only days before suddenly cried out for His death. He was beaten in public and mocked and spit on.

Jesus' tormentors weren't just trying to kill Him; they were also trying to humiliate Him, to make Him feel broken and alone. And there was no lonelier place to be. For what had to seem like an endless stretch of time, even God turned His back on His Son. With His last breath, "It is finished," Jesus took on the greatest sin and pain of humanity. The road to the cross was excruciating, both physically, emotionally, spiritually and mentally.

Jesus chose to go through all of that so God would not turn His back on me and you. He died in our place to offer us living water that gives us life abundant (even life that comes out of our tragedy and sorrow) and life eternal. He gets what it's like to hurt down deep.

In our most trying moments of grief, we are held tightly in the arms of the One who overcame the world.

He Never Leaves Us Alone in the Deepest Places of Pain

Sam's well may have been deep, but Jesus was ready, and able, to meet her deep place. By the well, He reminds us of two gifts we carry with us at all times: His time and His presence.

In Hebrews 13:5, He tells us to be courageous, because He's not going anywhere. Jesus love isn't the kind of love that walks or walks away. Even in the garden, just before the soldiers came to arrest Him, His last thoughts were with us.

I discovered an incredible little treasure in God's Word when I was thinking about how living water fills up our deep places. Take a look at this verse in Ephesians:

> And I pray that you, being rooted and established in love, may have power, together with all the saints, to grasp how wide and long and high and *deep* is the love of Christ" (Eph. 3:17-18, emphasis added).

The Samaritan woman used the word "deep" to describe her well. *But God uses the word "deep" to describe His love.* There is no depth His love can't penetrate. There is nothing that can separate us from that love (see Rom. 8:38-39).

Jesus is the only One who can truly heal the deep places in our hearts. But He doesn't just give us Himself and His time. He also gives us each other.

"Rejoice with those who rejoice and mourn with those who mourn" (Romans 12:5).

He Gives Us Other Shoulders to Cry On

Katie and Paxton's friendship was particularly special to me because my best friend also happens to be my first cousin. We look nothing alike—Melanie is tall with dark hair and dark eyes, while I'm short with blue eyes and a constellation of freckles—but we share many other things in common. We have the same taste in clothes. We tend to like the same movies and books. Even now, when we don't live in the same town and our lives are in two different places, we can go for weeks without talking but still pick up right where we left off. There's never an awkward pause.

After my grandfather (not related to Mel) passed away, I knew I needed someone to cry with. First I called my brother. Then I called my best friend. She answered on the first ring (because she already knew) and did what best friends do: she just let me cry. Later, she drove to my house and took me to Sonic. I slurped my Cherry Coke and thought about how sweet it was that we could still be there for each other like that. Melanie was the one I woke up at a sleepover when I thought I heard something in the closet. We cried over guys together, worried about family together and grieved through some hard seasons together. We celebrate good news and dreams come true. And when it comes to loss, each of us carries the other one through.

That is exactly what God tells us to do when our friends are walking through deep places. We don't have to say anything. Just being there to comfort them will help them make it through.

We should never disengage from our friends and family, especially when we are hurting. Sam had disengaged from society, and I have a feeling that this lack of true friendship only added to her heartbreak. Accountability is a sure-fire way to avoid fake paperdoll life and embrace abundant life. And so is true friendship, the gritty say-it-like-you-mean-it-there-for-you-no-matter-what-friendship that God gives us.

While we're talking about leaning on people, it's important to mention the reality of help. God has gifted counselors and pastors with the compassion to walk with us through dark seasons. If you are going through a season of pain in your life, find someone with whom you can share your hurt. Talk to your parents, your pastor, your mentor or a Christian counselor who can give you some guidance and perspective. An incredible amount of maturity rests in the heart of a person who knows he or she cannot untangle grief on his or her own.

He Gives Us Renewed Purpose and Passion

I got a sweet email from a former Bible study girl the other day. She mostly talked about her mom, who was battling cancer, and how brave and beautiful her mom was, especially in the face of so much uncertainty. Clearly, "brave" and "beautiful" was a genetic trait in this family line. Her email was full of her candid responses to what was happening. Of course, she was afraid and sad, but she was also incredibly courageous. She said she knew God would allow her to use this experience in her life to encourage someone else. She said she hoped there would be a day when she could talk to someone else with a family crisis and be able to truly say, "I understand what you're going through."

Few things are more comforting than someone who can come up beside you, know what you are feeling, and say they have been where you've been and mean it.

It is nothing short of a miracle to me that we can grieve simultaneously and still comfort one another; that part of the healing process that happens in our own hearts comes when we reach out to others. As long as there is breath still left inside us, we have work to do here. Maybe some of the greatest work we do comes from choosing to love through, in spite of, and because of a place of incredible pain.

He Gives Us an Eternal Hope

An incredible love note is tucked into Revelation 7, a promise that drenches our hearts in hope when we're somewhere sudden dark and deep: "For the Lamb at the center of the throne will be their shepherd; he will lead them to springs of *living water*. And God will wipe away every tear from their eyes" (v. 17, emphasis added).

I love knowing the image of "living water" is associated with the place of heaven. Jesus offered living water to Sam there by the well, and then comes this mysterious glimpse of eternity where living water flows free. There really is a place of perfect peace. There are no more funerals there, no more goodbye hugs at airports, and no more broken hearts. The scars may last for a lifetime, but healing will come. Until we get there, we have the promise of God's permanent presence. We have life abundant and life eternal.

The One who waited by the well whispers victory over your broken heart. So cry, and grieve, and question. Get help to make it through. Lean into your friends. And take heart, for He has already overcome the world.

Held

The Christmas after Paxton's death, the entire student ministry (and various brave adults who apparently didn't need much sleep) boarded the rickety church bus for our annual trip to the mountains. Katie and her friends made T-shirts with one of Paxton's most infamous sayings ("It's all good!") and wore them on the same night to the conference. I sat in the row behind Katie, listening to the band perform on stage. The row in front of me was a long line of black T-shirts—"It's all good" glowed bright neon in the dark auditorium. Eventually, the band sang a song called "Praise You in the Storm," a song that came to mean so much to Katie and her family. I knew that song in particular reminded Katie of Paxton, and my heart broke for her.

What happened next took me by surprise.

Katie lifted her arms and started singing along. Her worship that moment embodied her life. She was still confused, hurt and lonely, but she was confident in the One who carried her through the deep. She would still miss Paxton every day for the rest of her life, but she would live her life and carry the love she knew to the ends of the world and back.

I knew then that I'd been wrong about Katie. She did far more than just survive.

Her deep and genuine love for God has kept spilling over in so many beautiful ways in her life. A leader, a prayer warrior, a prom queen and a born encourager, she recently turned her tassel and took a deep breath, readying herself for college. The week before her graduation, she received a scholarship named for her best friend. The legacy both girls were determined to leave will live on in Katie.

I may be a little biased, but I'm convinced she's going to change the world. The mental snapshot of Katie at her best friend's funeral, broken and hurt, is bookmarked in my heart with another precious picture of her at a concert, broken . . . but triumphant.

There are two beautiful pictures of love tucked into my memory when it comes to those girls. One is at a funeral; the other is at a worship service. Both are otherworldly and strangely beautiful. Both remind me of how tenderly God meets us at the deepest points of pain and holds us, and carries us, and comforts us. Both remind me that He never, ever walks away from us.

I've learned that no matter how much I try to buffer my heart against pain, I don't get to pick the parts of life I want to experience. Dark seasons come. It's a given. And when they do—

when tragedy changes life in a second, when addiction leaves us feeling enslaved, when words cut into our hearts like knives—Jesus waits for us right there at our deepest place of pain and offers a love deeper than all of it.

I have a new theory about all of these unlikely beautiful ordinary moments that keep getting caught in my mind. I wonder if all these pieces of beautiful are just the shadow of a Kingdom our human eyes aren't trained to see. I wonder if we get a taste of heaven sometimes, in love, in beauty, in music, in worship and in the gift of family.

"Now we see but a poor reflection as in a mirror," Paul writes in 1 Corinthians, "then we shall see face to face" (1 Cor. 13:12). I'm waiting in eager anticipation for the face to face. It's good to know that there's a place where my heart won't break anymore. That there's a place where starlight and sunsets are second rate because, even if none of that were there, the people I let go of here will be there. And *He* will be there. It's good to know that there is a place where I'll be able to physically stand before Jesus, a day when He will wipe all these tears away from my eyes. And I'll remember how He cried *with* me and how He carried me through. For now, I'm wondering around in shadows and reflections, committed to carry out the purpose He has for me in my generation. But I can't wait to be there with Him, at home in the arms that held me all my life—arms I'll finally get to feel.

For now, I laugh and I smile. I hold on and let go for a little while. When life hurts, I'm learning to refuse the paper mask, to rip it to shreds if I have to and grieve. I remember. And I wonder if someday the way the skies in heaven fill up with color I've never seen will remind me of something else—one little isolated moment of joy or pain down here.

And then, like Katie, I think we'll lift up our arms in praise. Because we'll know at some moments in our messy lives, especially when we weren't looking, we really did see and taste and touch and know the deep love of a holy God. At beginnings and endings and all the way through, He's not leaving. He's walking beside us until the face to face.

On that day, it's all good.

As He spoke He no longer looked to them like a lion;
but the things that began to happen after that were so great
and beautiful that I cannot write them. And for us this is the end of
all the stories, and we can most truly say that they all lived happily
ever after. But for them it was really the beginning of the real story.
All their life in this world and all their adventures in Narnia had only
been the cover and the title page: now at last they were beginning
Chapter One of the Great Story which no one on earth has read: which
goes on forever: in which every chapter is better than the one before.

C.S. LEWIS, FROM *THE LAST BATTLE*[2]

Confessions

Lord, it is so easy for me to hide behind a paper smile
when my heart is breaking. Thank You for not only seeing
my deep places of pain but also offering me living water.
Thank You for holding me when I cry. Thank You
for giving me so many shoulders to cry on. Help me to
keep my eyes fixed on You when I'm moving through deep
seasons of pain and loss. I know You still have a purpose for
me here. I know Your plans for me are good. I know You
won't let me go. And I am so very grateful.

Note

1. Walter C. Kaiser and Duane Garret, eds., *The Archaeological Study Bible* (Grand Rapids, MI: Zondervan, 2005), notes on John 4:6, p. 1726.
2. C.S. Lewis, *The Last Battle* (New York: Harper Collins, 1994), pp. 210-211.

One Perfect Gift

Jesus answered her, "If you knew the gift of God and who it is that asks you for a drink, you would have asked and he would have given you living water."

JOHN 4:10

"May I . . . could I . . . would you mind going away while I did?" said Jill. The Lion answered with a look and a very low growl and as Jill gazed at its motionless bulk, she realized that she might as well have asked the whole mountain to move aside for her convenience. The delicious rippling noise of the stream was driving her nearly frantic.
"Do you promise not to . . . do anything to me if I do come?" said Jill.
"I make no promise," said the Lion.
Jill was so thirsty now that, without noticing it, she had come a step nearer.
"Do you eat girls?" she said.
"I have swallowed up girls and boys, women and men, kings and emperors, cities and realms," said the Lion. It didn't say this as if it were boasting, nor as if it were sorry, nor as if it were angry. It just said it.
"I daren't come and drink," said Jill.
"Then you will die of thirst," said the Lion.
"Oh dear!" said Jill, coming another step nearer. "I suppose I must go and look for another stream then."
"There is no other stream," said the Lion.
C.S. LEWIS, FROM *THE SILVER CHAIR*[1]

The biggest present under the tree was mine, and I couldn't wait to rip it open.

White Christmas lights reflected starry off the silver paper, making the box seem even bigger than it was. Unfortunately, that was the year my parents got smart and started laminating my gifts in tape (in previous years, I had discovered that making a small rip at various corners and seams was beneficial in determining contents). I had to rely on other methods to figure out what was inside my giant box. Namely, the shake test.

The box was heavy—always a good sign. When I shook it, it sounded like there was more than one piece, which could be good or bad. Either it had several components, or I had shaken the thing so hard it broke. I pictured grand things in that box: a pink Barbie jeep like Melanie's, a set of *Baby-sitter's Club* books, maybe even my very own machine that made everlasting gobstoppers (like the one in *Willy Wonka*).

I saved the sparkling silver gift for last on Christmas Eve, because I knew it would be my favorite. What happened next will live in infamy in old home movies. I'm hoping you never have to sit through said home movie, but if you do, the scene would play out like this: I sit on the last step, nervous and excited, fidgeting back and forth, playing with a tangle of my permed hair. I am already smiling as I contemplate where the everlasting gobstopper machine will fit in my room. Chase opens his gift first, and I feign interest, but secretly I am only anticipating the moment it is my turn to rip into my gigantic box. When I think my heart will explode from anticipation, my dad says, "Okay, Nat. Go for it."

I steady myself. I take a deep breath. I pick up the box (it's *so* heavy!). I finally find a small opening in the epidermis of clear tape.

I slowly rip the paper off my package.

And I realize that my parents have wrapped my huge wonderful gift in a hairdryer box. This is no big deal, I decide. Clearly, the box is just a random box big enough to hold the best Christmas present ever. I tear off more paper. Then I realize the box has never been opened. I sigh, flinging the last piece of paper off, and say (with a bundle of fake enthusiasm), "Wow. A hairdryer."

To be fair, I needed a hairdryer (or maybe I just needed a hair stylist to tell me to stop frying my hair with perms). I had just let my imagination get a bit carried away. I still shake and speculate on Christmas, trying to figure out what's in the box with my name on it. Hairdryer and all, I've been given some pretty sweet gifts. My family has never been into throwing down obscene piles of cash for Christmas presents, but the gifts (usually) tend to mean something special. In fact, my favorite gifts are usually the ones that don't plug in, don't cost much and don't always even get wrapped.

Paintings, funky handmade jewelry, used books, concert tickets, mixed CDs and even a trash sculpture and a bobblehead doll in my likeness are all safely tucked away in my old room. All of them touched my heart, because the giver really knew me and really put thought into how much I would like it. Whether it was based on an inside joke or a personal experience we shared, something about those gifts was endearingly sweet.

One year for Christmas, my Granny gave me a stack of poetry books. Gran was a tremendous lover of literature and could quote writers like Poe and Browning with flawless cadence. One of my favorite memories with her is sitting in my bedroom, listening to the rain pelt down hard against the trees outside while she quoted "Annabel Lee" from memory. Usually, Gran just gave me money for Christmas, but that year she gave me books full of poetry. She didn't even wrap them. Some of the books she gave me were classics. Others I'd never heard of, the work of new poets sharing their heart with the world. The best part of the gift was that she made notes on her favorite poems. One poem reminded her of watching her mom hang clothes on the line. Another reminded her of running through the high green hills behind her house as a little girl. In every book, one phrase remains scrawled across the front page: "Love Gran." Pure poetry.

She passed away the next year, and the books became like treasures to me. I trace my finger around her scribbled letters and picture her writing inside each copy. More than a book, she gave me little snippets of stories and memories. Her gift reminds me of the bright legacy she left behind. The gift comforts me when I miss her.

Gifts like that are truly unforgettable.

I guess it's no wonder my heart skipped a beat when Jesus said He had a gift for the Samaritan woman. "If you knew the gift of God," He says to her there by the well. I wondered how I could have heard Sam's story so many times and missed that word: *gift*. It wasn't the kind of gift she could fit in a box or tie up with a silky red bow. It was wrapped in mystery and beauty, bound by grace.

At the very beginning of their conversation, she had no clue what the gift even was. Jesus tells her if she did—if she knew the gift of God and who He was—she wouldn't be running to empty wells in her life, trying to get water out of them. She would be running to Him with everything inside her; everything she had for the one gift that would bring her fulfillment like no other.

Understanding—and accepting—the gift of God has the potential to change us from the inside out. Our paperdoll world offers so many gifts; some version of life beautifully packaged and put together with our name on it. It's just that those gifts are never as good as we think they will be. The gift at the well is different. It is life—abundant and eternal life—that flows down into the deepest corners of our paper hearts.

This is the gift that makes all others pale in comparison. This is the gift that sets us free from the wells to which we feel bound. And I have a feeling that once Sam realized what the gift really looked like lived out in a life, that hot dry day by the well felt like Christmas morning.

Discovering the Gift of God

Zoom back in on the scene at the well. Sam is confused, because Jesus has asked her for a drink. This makes no sense, because he's a man. And it gets even more confusing when He says, "If you knew the gift of God and who it is that asks you for a drink, you would have asked him and he would have given you living water" (John 4:10).

The Samaritan woman is thinking on a practical level. Jesus has nothing with which to draw water. The well is burrowed hundreds of feet into the ground. "Where can you get this living water?" she asks. This is when Jesus makes a powerful connection in her life, and our lives, about what *living* water truly is:

Everyone who drinks this water will be thirsty again,
but whoever drinks the water I give him will never thirst.
Indeed, the water I give him will become in him a spring
of water welling up to eternal life (v. 13).

Paul echoes that sweet truth in a no-frills explanation in the book of Romans. "The wages of sin is death," he writes, "but the gift of God is eternal life in Christ Jesus our Lord" (6:23). This was the greatest gift of all: no boxes, no ribbons, no twinkling lights, but eternal life through Jesus Christ. And Jesus wasn't just extending this gift to the elite and well rehearsed in Sam's community. He was offering eternal life to *her*.

Now, if Sam's culture was anything like ours, there were probably about a thousand different opinions of what happens after death. As much as we try to avoid thinking about endings, we can't help it. National tragedies make us wonder about what happens next. Sitting around with our girlfriends the night before graduation thinking about birthday parties we had when we were 7 and the butterflies we had in our stomachs when we were 17 can make us think about how fast time moves. I don't know who said "time flies when you're having fun," but I've learned it flies whether we're having fun or not. Years and days move at a crazy pace, and life keeps tossing us situations that make us think of what happens next. Jesus makes it abundantly clear in His Word. Heaven is a real place. It is real and permanent and amazing. But there is only one way to get there, and that's through Jesus Christ.

We can't buy our way in (see Eph. 2:8), or earn our way in, or even bring a wheelbarrow full of clothes and pottery shards. In the end, what matters is that we believed in Him.

Even if the sweetest gifts you have ever been given were all stacked in the same room, none of them would compare to the gift that God has given you in His Son. He offered this gift even though we didn't deserve it; offered it to Samaritans and small-town dreamers and city kids and college students. Grace is such an awesome and unfathomable concept, it's almost hard to write about.

But the gift goes even deeper than that.

Confessions of a Chronic Church Girl

While I never particularly cared for school (don't get me wrong, I'm grateful for my education—I just didn't like getting up early or doing math), I loved church on Sunday. I don't even remember the first time I went to my home church, but it was my church from that day to the day I moved 20-something years later. I know that plenty of people grow up with bad images of the church and how they've been hurt there, and I'm very grateful that my experience was different.

The people were (and still are) passionate, loving people. They were the kind of people who put bags of garden vegetables on someone else's front porch—just because. They taught Sunday School, did repairs and planned events without getting paid. They were there to comfort me when life went haywire. They were also hilarious (which is a perk). My church had a great emphasis on missions, so I was exposed to their giving nature early on. In fact, they helped me go on my first overseas missions trip. When I was little, I also had many talented Sunday School teachers who made the Bible seem alive and beautiful. I would have faked a cold to stay out of school every day if I could have, but church was different. I liked being there. It felt like home to me.

After watching a passion play at a church in Lexington (a building my church would have fit in three times over), I decided I wanted to make Jesus my life. I'd grown up seeing pictures of Him in Sunday School books, but something about seeing the story in 3D and watching Him "die" floored me. I was overwhelmed when I realized that He did that for me. Even then I knew that in the eyes of the world I was mostly a nobody, but in His eyes I was worth loving. I knew being a Christian wasn't just about being a church girl on Sundays. I knew it meant believing He died on the cross for my sins and that His grace gave me eternal life. It meant sharing that love with the world. I wanted to live for Him. I was confident that He was the most perfect gift I had ever, and would ever, know. Love rocked my nine-year-old universe.

By high school, I was still a chronic church girl. I nervously asked my pastor if I could teach a Sunday School class for fifth and sixth graders (which he excitedly let me do). I read my hot pink Bible under the willow tree in my yard. The stories I loved as a little girl were just as applicable and important to my 16-year-old world. I filled prayer journals with notes on anything and everything that was swirling in my heart: a sick grandparent, a boy I had a crush on, a dream so huge I was afraid to share it with anybody, a Geometry test I was 99.9 percent certain I would bomb. High school was confusing and weird and fun and awful all at the same time, but it was a sweet time in my walk with the Lord. I had many more questions than I did when I was nine, but my relationship with God meant more to me.

Then came college. Instead of getting involved in my church, I "church hopped." One weekend I went to a church with a great worship service. The next weekend I didn't feel like driving as far, so I went to a church nearby that had a cool pastor. Church was more hypothetical than a specific people or place. My time in God's Word was mostly limited to class discussions and Bible study. Occasionally I still read it on my own, but it didn't ignite my heart the way it once did. And because I went to a Christian college where all of my friends believed what I believed, I settled into an awkward pattern of rote faith. The passion I'd carried for years started to lose its fizz.

The summer before my senior year, I found my hot pink Study Bible from high school in my closet. I sat down on the floor and thumbed through the pages. I looked at Jeremiah 29:11-13, which was highlighted in yellow, underlined in black and noted on the side with a smiley face. I knew the verse by heart, but the last part resounded in a new way: "You will seek me and find me when you seek me with all your heart" (Jer. 29:13).

At some point, I realized the reason for the disconnect: I was no longer living the gift. Christ had sealed my place in heaven with His death on the cross and I had eternal life, but I was no longer inviting Him into the dailyness of my life. Life was more routine than abundant.

Christianity isn't built on some perpetual checklist about how many times we go to church, or how much money we give, or how much we serve in the community, or how many Bible studies we attend (or lead). The point is love. I can see seasons in my life when I walked with God out of pure, awestruck, simple love. I don't know how else to describe it; I was simply in love with the person of Jesus Christ. I wanted to love Him back with everything inside me. Other seasons, I approached my faith standoffish and awkward, just a paperdoll in tabbed-down church clothes.

In those seasons, I was missing the gift.

The way Jesus describes living water clues me in: He offers water "welling up into eternal life." Jesus didn't come to earth and die just to have us with Him for eternity (though that would certainly be more than enough if He had). He offers us the gift of His love, His presence and His peace in our everyday, ordinary lifetimes. He gives us a purpose to fulfill here and now. He offers guidance through His Word and gives us messages to carry in our present reality. "I have come that they may have life, and that they may have it more abundantly (John 10:10, *NKJV*).

Paperdolls are all about abundance. To me, it conjures up images of birthday parties full of tigers and cakes made of gold dust and people who have 28,000 "friends" on their social networking sites. It elicits images of celebrities on TV who show us their garage, which looks more like a car lot. It makes me think of how many messages a person has in his or her yearbook or how many text messages someone sends. And then I realize how bizarre it all is.

The abundant life Jesus offers is not fickle like that. It isn't attached to what we own or accomplish. It's not made of paper. It is eternal life, and it is life that feels real. It is comfort and joy and peace and relationships that mean something. Something can change in our hearts.

So, at this point by the well, I had to push the pause button and ask myself a question: *Am I living an* abundant *life?* Yes, I have asked Jesus to take Lordship over everything in and about me. I know His sacrifice on the cross was for me and that it was made so I wouldn't have to make it. I know I have eternal life (see John 5:24).

But I'm missing the gift if I'm not *living* an abundant life.

Legless Theology

One of my required classes in graduate school was a class on how to study the Bible. I was intimidated as soon as I walked in the door. Everybody else looked so collegiate and scholarly with their tiny computers already powered up in front of them. I could picture them sitting around reading Thomas à Kempis for fun while playing chess and listening to classical music, making smart jokes only their smart friends could understand. I didn't fit. I think infomercials are weirdly funny. I appreciate classical music but also (embarrassingly) know how to line dance. I like to read novels. And when my friends and I hang out, our conversations are about everything from God to reality television to how much milk it takes to get cereal to its desired level of crunchiness.

Although I was intimidated beyond belief, I knew the first night of class that I was going to love it. It was three hours long, packed full of notes and information . . . and I still gobbled it up. The work was even more intense than I imagined, but it was a good kind of intensity—the kind that left me exhausted in a good way. Every Wednesday night, I downed a double latte and searched through passages of text. Word by word, fragment by fragment, I kept scanning familiar stories for something I hadn't seen before. We poured over each word.[2] We took out the numbers and read the whole passage in context. We talked about what the "therefore" was there for and what was happening in that culture when those words were written.

It was pretty exciting to flip through dictionaries to find the Greek meaning of a word. I felt like the archaeologists on TV who find old maps and travel all across the globe looking for buried treasure. I scanned the text for new clues about a people and a culture and, more importantly, about the God I love. The most brilliant woman ever born could spend her whole life studying about God and still never come close to understanding His mind. I realize that. But I felt as if I were learning something new about His character.

Then, ever so slowly, the churchy paperdoll started slipping back in. I knew something was off when I wrote a paper about a passage in the Bible and had no clue what the verse actually said. I was in my car driving toward school when the verse got caught in my mind, and I realized, for the first time in a week of putting that paper together (who am I kidding . . . it was an hour or two), that the instruction in that specific passage resonated with a particular relationship in my life. I wasn't doing anything about it. I knew what the Word said, I just wasn't fitting it to my situation.

I knew God wanted me to engage Him intellectually and emotionally. I knew it was essential to study the Bible and know what it says. But there was a tremendous disconnect for me, because even in reading it, I was not applying it.

In the span of a semester, I read a load of Bible verses; beautiful ribbons of words that seemed to curl off the page. But I didn't try to bind those words to the life I was living. I had this gift in my hands—a Bible people in other countries die trying to procure, a gift that showed me how to live my life well and right—but I wasn't experiencing it at all. I was walking around with a legless theology, spouting truths I didn't really believe to be true.

"Do not merely listen to the word, and so deceive yourselves. Do what it says" (James 1:22).

Sam knew plenty about religion. She even knew a little bit about the coming Messiah. But she didn't know Jesus. He had extended a gift to her that day at the well: the gift of eternal life. But He extended another gift as well: abundant life. And that gift would be so much better than any well she'd gone to for love before.

I think that's one of the most tragic marks of a paperdoll: living a life that is flat on a page and not really living at all. Living is engaging in worship, being part of a community of people and discovering how your passion can impact the world for good. It is choosing to do the right thing in a situation, even when you are the only one doing it. It's choosing a high standard of holiness over a paper standard of instant gratification.

It has everything to do with unconditional love, and bright imagination, and intense compassion. It is choosing to believe relationships (not mountains of junk) make life sweeter. It is engaging the God of the universe daily, opening your whole heart to His love and direction, dreaming dreams that will bring Him glory, knowing He will write a beautiful story from your messy life. Abundant life is scary and intimidating and amazing.

No wonder Jesus compared His love to a fountain. Sam and her people would have been familiar with three water sources in particular: a cistern (which was a hole in the ground full of stagnant water), a well (wells weren't in high abundance there), and a fountain. Fountains were free-flowing streams with no end. They were constant. And Jesus is constant.[3]

Living in the Fullness

I know what I see when I look in my mirror. I see a girl who is still becoming. She's unsure of what she's good at. She's unsure where she'll be in 5 or 10 years. She's a little bit jealous of friends who have their lives figured out. She likes her freckles, but she's self-conscious about her nose. She would wear jeans every day of her life if she could. She's prone to daydreaming and overanalyzing. She's more than a little bit clumsy. She's ordinary, ultimately. And she is acutely aware of her paperdoll heart. She can think of many places she's gone looking for acceptance that left her feeling empty.

I so often forget I'm made in the image of God; made with a heart only He can fill completely. I forget He sees so much more in me than I see. He sees all the places I've messed up, but more than that, He sees the woman I can become. He knows the potential in me. He loves all of me. He knows the gifts He's put inside me. He knows the capacity I have to love. He knows what I'm good at and where I'm weak. And if I'm willing, He will use me.

The same was true with Sam. God knew about her past. He knew about her broken relationships. He knew why she was there alone at the well. But He was about to give her a huge message to carry to the world anyway. He saw something more than what she saw or what the people in her village saw.

He saw past the paper.

We're just ordinary girls, but wrapped in the grace and love of an extraordinary God, we have the potential to do great things. If we are really living out the gift of God in our lives, our hearts and our worlds can change in amazing ways:

- In place of our endless pursuits of physical perfection, we are filled with a picture of real true beauty. We get to walk in confidence, because we belong to Christ.

- In place of endless pursuits of romance (which typically end in a string of broken hearts), we are given the courage to wait and have relationships built on integrity. Jesus offers us a love that is permanent and real.

- In place of bitterness and rejection, we are filled with a spirit of anticipation, hope and peace.

- Instead of an obsessive desire for status and notoriety, we become women determined to leave a legacy that outlasts our lifetime.

- In place of perpetual busyness, we are filled with a spirit of urgency to go and share His love with a lonely world.

- In place of anxiety, we are given His perfect peace.

- In place of self-absorption, we are filled with purpose, passion and an others-focused way of living that seems completely counter to culture. Materialism is replaced by passionate world consciousness.

- In place of our whiny apathetic groan, we're filled with a courageous cry for change.

- Instead of carrying a victim mentality the rest of our lives, we become passionate advocates for the hurting.

- In place of seclusion and isolation, we are given the courage to go back into the community and into the world with confidence and compassion.

- And instead of becoming another cultural pawn, a lookalike paperdoll who is nothing more than a walking billboard for materialism, we become true worshipers of the living God. We understand that we are image bearers of the Divine, and so we shine.

I think something incredible floods over our soul when we walk into the world carrying the gift of God. There's a reason Jesus used a water metaphor to describe all that. A fountain is free flowing and eternal. The love we pull from wells, even the prettiest wells, is a drippy garden hose compared to the love of God.

A Different Kind of King

In his book *Twelve Extraordinary Women*, John MacArthur makes a great observation about Sam's conversation by the well. Messianic expectation was huge at this point in history, but, just like the Bible foretold, even some of Jesus' own people didn't think that He was the Messiah. MacArthur thinks it's at this point in the conversation that Sam gets a clue about who Jesus is:

There was a subtle hint of Messianic expectation in his words, and she got it . . . is it not significant that this Samaritan woman, born and raised in a culture of corrupt religion, had the same messianic hope as every other godly woman in Scripture?[4]

"I know that Messiah . . . is coming," she says. "When he comes, he will explain everything to us" (John 4:25). These words, according to MacArthur, strongly hint at the fact that she believes Jesus is the Messiah. And Jesus, ever the rebel mold-breaker, tells a *Samaritan woman* by the well the greatest truth the world will ever hear: "I who speak to you am he" (v. 26).

I wonder how that realization of who Jesus really was compared with what she had been taught the Messiah would be. I wonder if she'd been expecting a fierce warrior. I wonder if she'd imagined a parade of warhorses riding against the horizon, announcing his entrance. If so, she would have been surprised by the man waiting at the well. Knowing Him, hearing His voice, talking to Him forever sealed in her mind who the Messiah was.

We live in a culture with so many interpretations of God. The world keeps looking for a Savior in all the wrong places. History is marked by men and women who justified cruelty and pain in the name of God. I think sometimes the gift of God is hard for us to understand or live out because our image of Jesus is clouded.

We picture Jesus like the parent who walked away, or like the boyfriend who fell in love with someone else, or like the guy who never noticed us, or like the church that made us feel rejected. Even Christianity can have a fake glitzy sheen to it sometimes, so it's easy to think that Jesus is like that, too—that maybe His favor only rests on the wealthy and articulate. We fall into the mistaken belief that He can only use us someday when we're older and better looking, more confident, and have it all figured out.

The only true Savior of the world is as indefinable and mysterious as He is loving and peaceful. He's not a divine gumball machine in the clouds, dishing out blessings when we perform well and tragedy whenever He feels like it. He's not a game-show God who reveals just enough of a dream to intrigue us and then deducts from the score as soon as we are wrong. He's not an infomercial God who dishes out scores of monetary blessings as soon as we accept His exclusive offer. He's not a mean God sitting in the clouds hurling lightening bolts at our every attempt to move. And He's not some enlightened guru in a robe who mumbles sayings that sound like something out of a stale fortune cookie.

Our human minds are incapable of comprehending the mind of God. All we have to go on is how He describes Himself in His Word.

He walked through the earth just like us, but He looked at the world through divine eyes—through eyes of compassion and love.

He spoke passionately about ending slavery and abuse.

He confused the daylights out of people when He revolutionized the concept of what the promised Messiah would be. His kingdom was never about glitter and glamour but about service and love.

He overlooked the most important and called out the little guy hiding in the tree. He bypassed the castles and sat down in the home of Mary and Martha. He liked having dinner with His friends. He loved His parents. He needed time alone with God the Father.

There was a romanticism about the way He spoke sometimes. He understood love at its most rare and beautiful and called the meek, lonely and troubled "blessed" in His tender soliloquy on the hillside.

He got angry and threw the tables over in the Temple because the materialism He saw there made Him sick. He cried when He experienced loss, and He celebrated with others. He was the consummate artist, carpenter and heart-mender. Instead of coming to judge and condemn, He came, so He tells us, to set the captives free (see Luke 4:18).

And there in the Garden of Gethsemane, with the weight of a broken world bearing down on His heart, He prayed for us. He marched to the cross and held His arms open wide and died there because He wanted us with Him in eternity, so that we wouldn't walk the earth alone. Life eternal. Life abundant.

He fought for me once and won my soul. But He says He fights my battles for me still. He says He's never leaving me. So, every day, He wins my heart. He is, truly, the most perfect gift.

> "We wrongly imagine that what we do for Christ is more important than what he did for us." — John MacArthur

When He becomes the center of my worship, my affection and my life, the way I live starts to change. I want the love of God to show in me. I want the love of God to flow out of my life into the world around me. What matters, He said, is that we love Him with all our hearts, souls, minds and strength—and that we love others. I want to carry that love into a lonely dark world. I want to live the gift with everything inside me. And I want His living water to flood my mind, heart and soul. Because when it does—when I get a true picture of His love against all these empty places I go looking for fullness—the fake, meaningless disguises start to crumble like a paperdoll in the rain.

Confessions

*Lord, if You came to earth just to save me,
that would have been enough. Thank You for coming
to give me life abundant, too. Thank You for covering me
with Your love. Thank You for sending Your Holy Spirit to
live inside me. As much as I am able this side of heaven,
I want to know You. I want to learn to love and serve like
You did. I want the world to see You in me.*

Notes

1. C.S. Lewis, *The Silver Chair* (New York: Harper Collins, 1994), pp. 22-23.

2. We literally poured over each word. My first assignment was to look at Acts 1:8 and find 20 things about that one verse in the Bible. The next week's assignment was to find 20 more facts about Acts 1:8. And then the next week . . .

3. The Gospel of John is a veritable literary flood. Jesus is baptized by (the other) John in the Jordan River (see 1:29). He changes water into wine (see 2:1-11). He heals a sick man beside the pool of Bethesda (see 5:1-18). He walks on water (see 6:16-21). And He meets up with our girl by the well.

4. John MacArthur, *Twelve Extraordinary Women* (Nashville, TN: Thomas Nelson, 2005), pp. 148-149.

8

Pianos and Paintbrushes

*Believe me, woman, a time is coming when you will worship
the Father neither on this mountain nor in Jerusalem.
You Samaritans worship what you do not know; we worship
what we do know, for salvation is from the Jews. Yet a time is
coming and has now come when the true worshipers will
worship the Father in spirit and truth, for they are the
kind of worshipers the Father seeks.*

JOHN 4:21-24

❀ ❀ ❀

*I wanted to find the place where the sunset dripped off the earth.
I wanted to touch the sky it left behind: a pale blue canvas smeared gray
and pink. I wanted to feel it like paint on my hand when I pull away.
I wanted to swing from the stars, one by one, and then skim over the
ocean and feel the water ripple beneath my fingertips.
But I could only watch. And I sat amazed.
I watched Your creation cry out to You, paint Your love
across the fading sky. I wondered how anything I could ever say,
or write, or sing could declare Your love like this. I found it
hard to believe I get to take all this so personally.
I hope my worship looks this beautiful to You.
Thank You for giving me an ocean that keeps curling around
my ankles, pulling me in deeper. Thank You for the stars that surround
me, scattered diamonds across the stage of the universe.
Thank You for loving me more than all of this.
Nothing compares to being near You, standing in Your shadow,
walking in Your light. From now on when the rocks and
the waves cry out to You, I will too.
I'll follow You to the end of the ocean, to the end of the earth,
and to the end of my heart.*

❀ ❀ ❀

A soft morning breeze pushed through the island. With it came so much of what I love about that piece of the world: soft pink petals blowing out of the trees, the smell of the ocean, and the warmth of the coming summer. I was driving with the windows down en route to the center of my favorite beach town. I had a simple goal in mind: to grab a milkshake at my favorite diner, walk toward the lighthouse and watch the water. I wanted to soak in every last ray of sunlight I could find before I headed back toward the mountains.

As soon as I opened my car door, I heard the familiar sounds of the pier: kids laughing while they played on the swing set, seagulls screaming overhead, and the gentle, constant roar of the ocean. I heard music, too, which is typical, but this wasn't some acoustic band playing outside the thrift store. This day, a church service was set up under a grove of shade trees. The song I heard playing was a familiar worship song, which was kind of ironic.

For weeks I'd been praying that God would teach me more about what it meant to be a true worshiper. It's that concept—*worship*—that really hooked me into Sam's story in the first place. It's not like it's some foreign concept to me. I was just beginning to see how, in some ways, it had lost some of its meaning in my life.

I'd been making a point of asking friends from different denominational backgrounds what worship meant to them. I asked them what they thought of when they heard the word; what was the first picture that popped up into their minds. The answers were varied. For some of them, worship was a weekly service for 20-somethings in a hipster section of Atlanta. The service is an adrenaline rush that's always packed out with people seeking God. It's moving and convicting and heartbreaking all in the same breath. For others, worship meant an old hymn or the image of people with their eyes closed in reflection—something more subtle, traditional or thoughtful. For some, worship brought to mind images of physicality or posture: people kneeling, people lifting their arms, people dancing. Pictures of worship included everything from bent knees to electric guitars to candlelight. Worship can be all of those things.

All the while, I was trying to determine what worship meant to me. Why does it feel so real and beautiful sometimes, but so fake at other times? The question was burning inside my heart.

So I paid close attention to the girl by the well.

At this point in our journey through Samaria, we've seen Sam engage Jesus in some serious (and amazing) conversation. We've watched the broken pieces of her heart come together as she realizes who He is. She's realized that she matters to someone. He's offered her this mysterious gift of living water. She has a hunch that Jesus is more than just a good man. There's an undercurrent of messianic expectation in Sam's culture, so the question may have been circling in her mind early on. For now, she thinks He's at least a prophet.

As soon as she makes this observation, the conversation takes another strange turn. Even though she believes Jesus to be a prophet, she doesn't talk to Him about the great mysteries of science. She doesn't ask about her future, or who she'll marry, or how many kids she'll have. There's something else burning on her heart that she wants to ask Jesus: what *worship* looks like in a life.

I'm so glad she asked.

Even though the Bible talks about worship (a lot), this is the only time Jesus mentions it directly. I want to know why it matters in this story and, in particular, I want to know why it should matter to me. Is there a way to do it "right"? A place it seems more fitting?

I'd asked plenty of people what worship meant to them and how it should look, but I didn't know if I'd really tried to think about what Jesus said about it. Worship, like writing, like love, like a real relationship with God, is one of those things I completely miss if I just read about it and ask about it but don't actually *do* it. Life is only flat on a page for paperdolls. For real girls, life is gloriously participatory.

So I didn't think twice about following the music away from the pier that day. And what I found was nothing short of extraordinary.

Spirit and Truth

I stopped where a band was playing an acoustic set under a canopy of moss-covered trees, the wild blue ocean stretching out behind them. With one look around, I knew I instantly liked the way beach dwellers did church. Nothing about this Sunday service was buttoned up or formal. People wore flip-flops, messy ponytails and sunglasses. A few kids were dancing to the sound of the guitar off in the corner. Another man was sitting at a table and listening intently with a cigarette curled in his left hand. Some people stood close to the front with their arms raised. Others were drifters, people who just happened to be nearby and followed the music, like I did.

I sat on a picnic table on the perimeter of the shade trees, my chin propped in my hand, mouthing the words to a song I knew by heart. Then I saw one of the most true, and beautiful, pictures of worship I've ever seen.

I first noticed an elderly man in a wheelchair. He sang every word of the song by heart. His chair was turned toward the band and his hands rested in his lap. But even as he sang, his eyes were watching white sails rip across the distant horizon. I wondered what his story was. Did he grow up here? Did he spend time out on the sea as a young man? Was that his idea of adventure once? I wondered if the ocean reminded him of God: wild but peaceful, constant but unpredictable.

Near him sat a middle-aged man in khaki shorts and a T-shirt. His elbows rested on the table, and he lifted one arm in the air as he sang the same words. His story wasn't as far along yet. I wondered if he was a local or a vacationer; if maybe he had stepped away from busy planning (or busy rest, as vacations so often become) to spend some time with God. I wondered if his place in the breezy shade reminded him of God's perfect peace.

Just then, a young woman walked up behind the two men. The sun and shadow illuminated her dark skin, and her hair blew around in the summer breeze. She lifted both her arms skyward, singing the same words to the God all three of them loved. She was young and beautiful. The gold and silver bangles on her arm made a pretty clinking sound when she raised her hands. She had a messenger bag draped around her shoulder that bulged at the side with books. She seemed so culturally savvy to me, like the kind of woman who could talk art and music and classic literature. The God to whom she sang was relevant to all of that; to every last drop of the life she led.

They were three different people at different places in life, but they each had one commonality: a God they adored. From the depths of their hearts, they cried out to Him. It didn't matter so much where they were, or how they were dressed, or even who was watching them. Their emotional responses were different, but they all engaged in a heartbreakingly real kind of worship. I instantly thought of Jesus' words to Sam there by the well: "God is Spirit, and His worshipers must worship Him in spirit and in truth" (John 4:24).

I had locked my arms around my chest at this point, not because I was cold, but because I felt as if my heart were about to explode. It's so easy for me to dismiss worship in my life, or forget what it looks like, or, perhaps most pathetically, to worship a pile of stuff (or even certain people) in place of God.

Maybe that's what I needed to see: worship that was completely directed toward the God of heaven and worship that was *true*. I needed to be reminded that worship isn't just about feelings or emotions. It isn't a secret locked in stained-glass Sundays or denominational preferences. I can lift paper arms into the air or keep them in my lap, and it won't matter. Even worship can be a paperdoll masquerade if my heart isn't wrapped up in the act as well.

Worship in spirit and truth has a mysterious kind of intimacy attached to it. It gets the focus off me and back on the God I love. Worship, when it is real, is liberating. There's a reason it came up in the conversation by the well and here in my heart for this season: worship has a way of setting paper hearts free.

If I can break out of this paper mold—if I can give my attention and adoration and affection back to the only One who truly deserves it—worship can be one of the most beautiful, intimate acts I will ever experience while I walk this earth.

Leading a Life of Extravagant Worship

Let's go back to the girl by the well and try to get a clearer picture of her surroundings in Samaria. We've pictured Jacob's well, burrowed deep into the ground. John also tells us that there were fields nearby ready for harvest. And towering over Sychar was a high mountain called Gerizim. This mountain held a very specific religious importance to the Samaritans.

Remember, Sam lived in a religious culture. Much like our world, there was plenty of bickering going on about the right way to do religion. One major argument (or if not a major argument, at least one that caught her interest) seemed to be about how to worship. The Jews and the Samaritans had very different ideas about *where* worship should occur.

For Sam's people, the "right" place was high on Mount Gerizim. In fact, if you were to ask them the first image that came to mind when they heard the word worship, they might have answered "the mountain." Or the view from the mountain. Or they might have said something like "tradition." Gerizim was where their parents and grandparents had worshiped for centuries.

This can be an important lesson for all of us: Having a legacy of faith stretching generations behind you can be an amazing thing, but there still comes a point when a girl has to embrace her faith as her own. Tradition is beautiful and meaningful and can teach us much about where we come from. But

God wants personal relationships with His girls. If the Samaritans understood worship in a context of place or tradition only, it's no wonder they were feeling a little bit flat.

For the Jews, the "right" place to worship was in the Temple in Jerusalem. To some extent, both groups were missing the point. Worship can happen in a cathedral or an elevator shaft and still be worship. The point isn't *where* the worship takes place but *who* is being worshiped. Jesus had much to say on the subject in His conversation by the well:

> Jesus replied, "Believe me, dear woman, the time is coming when it will no longer matter whether you worship the Father on this mountain or in Jerusalem. You Samaritans know very little about the one you worship, while we Jews know all about him, for salvation comes through the Jews" (John 4:21-22, *NLT*).

True worship is close to the heart of each of us who long to stand defiant against a paperdoll culture. Worship, when it is real, is distinctly beautiful. It comes out of the deepest core of a grateful heart. It floods our art, our decisions and our lives. Women who worship God just seem different. They walk differently. They can stand strong against a culture consumed by arrogance, greed and self-centeredness. True worshipers have a certain abandon in their relationships with Him and know their lives are all about *Him*.

Once we give our worship to the one true God and learn to worship Him in spirit and truth, it's hard to keep the paper façade in place.

Searching for Something Real

If you take a brief detour from the well and flip toward the book of Acts, you'll find yourself in the middle of another fantastic biblical scene. Paul is preaching a sermon in the city of

Athens. He begins by acknowledging how the Athenians (like
the Samaritans, like us) are a "religious people." But they (like
Sam's people, like us) are getting the real meaning of worship
all twisted. The jumping off point in Paul's sermon is just as
relevant for today as it was back then:

> Men of Athens! I see that in every way you are very reli-
> gious. For as I walked around and looked carefully at
> your objects of worship, I even found an altar with this
> inscription: TO AN UNKNOWN GOD. Now what you wor-
> ship as something unknown I am going to proclaim to
> you (Acts 17:22-23).

My own journey to the well keeps showing me how many
ways I have tried to bend my desire for God toward some kind of
fulfillment offered by my world. My heart is created to love, but
I come up empty when I try to find perfect love anywhere besides
Jesus. Reminders of the great tragedy of worshiping, and loving,
the wrong things haunt the story of humankind: from the fall in
the Garden of Eden, to the tombs of the Pharaohs, to this glittery
modern-day era (where golden cows come in clever marketable
disguises). History is full of monuments to unknown gods.

Some of us worship celebrities. We know everything about
them: their birthdays, their favorite foods and the names of
their kids. We talk about them like they're our friends. We buy
the socks they wore to a nightclub for $4,000 on eBay. We cry
and scream in sheer joy at the thought of touching them. We
spend our free time reading about them. In dire circumstances,
we even try to craft our bodies to look like them. Some of us
worship boyfriends and crushes. We would do anything to make
them stay. We think about them with every waking thought.
We're willing to give away our hearts and our bodies at the prospect of being near them just for a little while.

Some of us worship wealth, or at least the illusion of it. We
refuse to buy anything without a fancy label sewn in the back.

Our cell phone has to be the newest and coolest version. Our laptop is state-of-the-art brand-new. The car we drive is top of the line and fully loaded. Everything we own, in our minds, becomes an extension of who we are. The list goes on and on.

I do not want my life to be hallmarked by monuments to unknown gods or to temporary fillers that give me momentary love or satisfaction. I don't want my life to be hallmarked by the worship of a person or a thing. When I die, I don't want people at my funeral to say, "She had lots of cool stuff." Living a life full of empty worship is far more tragic than dying.

Jesus tells Sam that yes, the Jews do have one particular aspect of worship figured out: they know the God they worship. Salvation is coming from the Jews, because He is a Jew. The Samaritans don't know the God they worship.

We don't have to look any further for the One who deserves all our worship and all our praise. We may still be up in the air about some of the major points in our lives: what we'll do someday, who we'll marry, what city we'll call home. But, like the Samaritan woman, there's one area we must finalize right now. We have to learn to direct our worship to the only One who deserves it.

I know Who is worthy of my praise. By the ocean, by myself, with a group of people, and by the well, God is teaching me a few things about real worship.

Real Worship Is Worshiping God with My Heart, Mind, Soul and Strength

Several years ago, I took my Bible study girls to a conference in Lexington. In almost every way, the trip was typical. We stopped for bathroom breaks at every exit. We talked about guys. We sang along ridiculously loud with the radio. We talked about guys. We ate our weight in Twizzlers and Dasani. We talked about guys. We ordered pizza in the hotel and tried to jump on the elevator just before it landed so we could go airborne (which they claimed was possible, but I'm still not convinced).

Finally, we pulled into the parking lot of the huge church where the conference was being held. Our home church was significantly smaller (it was located beside a giant cow field), and I'll never forget one girl's expression as she stared wide-eyed at the massive building, sighed, and said, "that looks like a mall."

This church felt different in another way, too. Within an hour, we were worshiping God with girls from several different denominational backgrounds. Our student ministry embraced contemporary worship. We had a band. We knew all the songs the worship leader sang. But at this event, several girls were dancing around near the stage (which was not a commonality back home). One of my sixth grade girls leaned over, her brown eyes sparkling, and said, "Are we allowed to do that?"

To which I replied, "Heck yeah, you're allowed to do that."

Much like her, I'm learning that the way I worship will not always look the same. Worship is an act of love and adoration, a personal genuine response to God. It's how I love God back, and there are many ways I can show Him I love Him.

Worship doesn't look the same for every person. There isn't just one way to worship. Not only is it not about a place but, thankfully, it also doesn't hinge on one denomination. Jesus made it a point to let Sam know that worship wasn't just a Jewish thing. And it wasn't just a Samaritan thing. It wasn't really a big deal whether they were in the Temple or on a mountain.

In the same way, it doesn't matter if we're worshiping in a big church or a small one. What matters is that we are genuine in our worship to God.

Sometimes my reaction to worship is to lift my hands. Sometimes I stay in my seat. Sometimes I want to be on my knees with my face to the ground. What I do physically when I worship isn't the issue; it's what I do with my heart. If the way I physically respond to worship isn't an extension of what is going on in my heart, then it isn't real. I'm just a paperdoll with raised hands.

Genuine worship doesn't hinge on externals. It doesn't matter if worship brings up images in our mind of full bands or acoustic guitars (or both things). It isn't about the music. A moment of worship may happen with no music present. It may happen at a praise service. We can raise our hands or sit in a chair or be on our knees on the ground.

Worshiping God in spirit and in truth is so real because it engages all of us. I love this quote from *Integrity's iWorship Daily Devotional Bible*: "Worship is not a spectator sport; it's full contact spirituality."[1] It is about engaging our heart, mind and spirit in praising God.

Real Worship Is Living Out My Love, Awe and Adoration of God

As I grow in my relationship with Christ, worship remains dear to my heart because it hinges on pure, reverent love. One of the first things I notice about the true worshipers in the Bible is *how* they approached God. There was a distinct reverence to who He was.[2] Worship leader Chris Tomlin says, "You will never worship anything you don't see as bigger than yourself."

> "Therefore, I urge you brothers, in view of God's mercy, to offer your bodies as living sacrifices, holy and pleasing to God—this is your spiritual act of worship" (Romans 12:1).

That truth was ingrained in the hearts of men and women in the Bible. When I walk in the awareness of the awesome magnitude of God—of His grace, mercy and love—my worship seems to be more true. It isn't just something I do on Sundays or something I do when I'm celebrating. Worship becomes an opportunity to love Him for who He is every day. Worship is a place where my genuine, reverent love for God meets with an awestruck awareness of His holiness, love and goodness.

Worship is where love and respect ignite. Worship is how I love Him back.

Because loving and being loved are my two favorite things in the world, I can think of no more meaningful experience than worship. "These are the worshipers God seeks," says Jesus. And once we get an awareness of how sweet it is to be pursued by a holy God, our lives are never the same.

I want to be the kind of woman who leads a life of extravagant worship.

Living a Life that Sings

As I learn how to worship God in spirit and in truth, I want to be intentional about how I worship God with my life. While the following list isn't exhaustive, here are a few ways I want to love God back for how He loves me.

I Want to Worship Through My Art and My Creativity

Chase and I recently watched a concert clip of Coldplay that began with scruffy-faced lead singer Chris Martin singing a song called "Clocks." Chase is an incredible musician, so he appreciated the finer notes of the performance I didn't even notice. I was just caught up in the sweeping emotion of it all. I wish I could write the way Chris Martin plays piano. He gets so absorbed in what he's doing. It really seems like an art form for him, not just another song he's sung a thousand times. He sings while his hands move furiously across the keys. He can barely stay seated (and sometimes he doesn't). The end result is beautiful chaos. What he does isn't effortless, but it is beautiful. In every song, you get the feeling he's giving his best performance, a raw glimpse into his heart.

I want my worship to be like that as well. I want to offer God my best art and my creativity. I never want to stop being inspired by my Creator. Songwriters, painters, actors, poets, musicians, carpenters and every other artist has that potential—to wrap their art around an emotion, around a certain piece of this messy, beautiful life, and acknowledge the One who thought it all up. I've noticed that most creative types feel close to God when they create. Whether your method of creation is a piano or a paintbrush, a banjo or a blue ink pen, use it to worship the Lord.

I Want to Worship When I'm Alone

I heard a worship pastor talk about one of his least favorite phrases. He said it always makes him cringe when someone says they come into church on Sunday morning and finally feel as if they're experiencing worship for the first time all week. The statement breaks his heart because, ultimately, we have the opportunity to worship God anywhere. In fact, if we don't take the time to worship Him in private, we are missing out on something beautiful.

Like any relationship, my relationship with God grows deeper when I'm intentional about being alone with Him. I'm learning it's important for me to take time, even apart from the time I spend in Bible study and prayer, to worship God. Whether I'm in the floor in my living room, curled up on my bed or driving in my car, there's a particular sweetness to solo worship that I would be crazy to miss out on.

I Want to Worship Him with Other Believers

Throughout the Bible, God makes a point of pulling people into community. We get some tender alone time with Him as well, like Sam did, but we also get to lock arms with other people to experience this mess of life together. Simon and Garfunkel may have been content being rocks and islands, but for the rest of us, life can get pretty lonely if we're always flying solo. It's easy to go paperdoll when you think the world only revolves around the island of you.

Just as we're called to experience life together and serve God together, doing worship together is an incredible privilege.

I love standing in a room and hearing a praise chorus rise in unison. I remember there's something that God wants to teach me about His character through these people. I remember that I'm called to love and serve them. No matter how many differences we have or how many petty arguments we get into, we stand united in our love for the One who waited by the well.

I Want to Worship in Joy and Celebration

I can't help but think that the God who thought of joy, surprise, excitement and love would want to celebrate with us. When good things happen, I'm learning to go to Him first, not last, and spaz out a little bit in His presence. Sometimes, a perfect sunrise (that wakes me up before my annoying alarm clock), or a bit of good news, or a phone call from a relative, or a good medical report, or a new opportunity sends my heart soaring. I want to thank Him for all that goodness and celebrate it with Him. No celebration is sweeter than the one He's in on.

I Want to Worship in My Sorrow and Confusion

I used to just link worship with Sunday mornings and celebratory times. In the Bible, there are plenty of pictures of worshipers loving on God when victory is finally at hand. But another beautiful picture of worship emerges when we see people calling out to God in their sorrow. One such picture comes from the book of Job.

On what may have started out like any other day, Job is crushed by tragedy. A messenger comes to find him and tells him that all of his kids have been killed in a horrible accident. Nothing about the news seems right or rational. Job loves the Lord. He loves his family. He seems to be just a normal guy trying to do good. But when he receives news of this mind-numbing tragedy, this is how he responds: "At this, Job got up and tore his robe and shaved his head. Then he fell to the ground in worship" (Job 1:2).

Job's worship wasn't some fake cheesy show for his friends to see. He didn't do it with his arms raised as he danced in circles and sang happy songs. He didn't smile and say, "Well, at least they're in a better place." On this particular day, Job's worship came from the ground. He tasted dirt and tears as he cried out through his pain to the God he loved. He was physically and emotionally distraught by this horrific news and yet, even then, his heart moved into a place of worship.

Worship is an involuntary reaction of the soul's longing for Christ's return. Even in our anger and confusion, there is something about worship that comforts us during times of pain. God even points out a precious fact in His Word: He reminds us that Job did not sin in accusing God of wrongdoing. (I maintain that God wants us to be genuine in our feelings and thoughts. He's big enough for the questions.) He asked "why?" and poured out his frustration and worshiped God at the same time. Sorrow and worship are not exclusive. In fact, sometimes they move through our hearts so tightly bound that we can't pull them apart.

As we keep that mental image of Job worshiping from the ground fresh on our minds, it's interesting to look again at the picture of God's people worshiping in the book of Revelation. We get to worship Him together in that beginning. We get to let our voice mingle with thousands of other voices: those we've loved and lost, great heroes we've only read about, great heroes we've never heard of, and all the angels that circle around the throne and praise God. Worship reminds us that this isn't the end of the story. This isn't even the best part of the story. The song we sing facedown on the ground through tears, in the mud and with broken hearts is just the beginning of a symphony that is building, rising and swelling into eternity.

I have a feeling we're going to love the way the song sounds up there.

I Want to Worship Him in the Midst of His Creation

My friend Sarah and I like to joke that a perfect day would involve riding four-wheelers and getting pedicures. We're only partially joking. I grew up in the mountains near a national park chock full of paths to explore and rivers to raft and a host of other outdoor activities. I've never been much of an outdoorsy girl but, like even the girliest girls I know back home, I have a deep appreciation of nature. Mountains make me feel at home. In fact, one of my favorite places in my hometown is the back porch that belongs to my friends Tom and Eve (who graciously loan their porch out to me when I need some time away from the world). When I'm there, I can count at least 13 rows of smoke-gray mountains rippling off toward the horizon. I read psalms about God's magnitude and wonder and feel so alive and excited. I also feel so very small. And so very loved by God.

The Bible is full of God's kids singing about His creation. David, in particular, was a fan of the great outdoors. He felt close to God when he realized the magnitude of God's handiwork (and really, if Mount Everest is something God created, how big and amazing must the mind of God be?). When I'm high up in the mountains, or standing on the rim of the ocean, or driving through flat lands with a sky so big and blue I want to get lost in it, I remember God is bigger than I will ever fully comprehend. I realize how completely out of control I am. The world is far bigger than me, big enough to swallow my dreams whole. But I'm also reminded of how God surrounds me with His love. He's walking me through this earth. I remember that no situation is too big for Him to handle.

I love getting away and being alone with Him from some corner of His gorgeous world. And there are so many corners of this world to explore; so many places I can share with Him alone. There are so many beautiful moments of worship I can engage in during my life. I don't want to miss another one.

One Song Rising Toward the Punched-tin Sky

In the Old Testament, God gives a stuttering Egyptian-raised Hebrew named Moses a powerful message to carry to Pharaoh.

One particular part of that message is a fairly well known sentiment, made famous by a white-haired Charlton Heston, and a giant talking pickle, among others. "Let my people go," Moses says. But until I started looking at worship in the Bible, I didn't really notice the last part of that message. Each time we find God's command to Pharaoh in Exodus to "let my people go," the command always ends with the words, *"so that they may worship me."*

I think it's incredible that worship is associated with *freedom*. Worship has the power to move me out of paper pursuits and into the arms of a real and loving God. Unlike all those other faulty places I try to dish out my love and affection, God returns my love far more than I deserve or understand. Even though worship is all about Him, it's inevitable that I feel loved in the process—and that I feel free. Suddenly, I'm no longer a slave to paperdoll standards. I'm not defined by how much I weigh, or what guy I'm crazy about, or where I go to school. My focus on me, and where I'm not enough, dissolves away when I focus on God.

Worship is our freedom song, and I think Sam got that, too. I don't know why worship was on the forefront of her mind that particular day, but I have a feeling she was ready to experience something real. She was aching to get her hands on some living water. I think she was ready to wrap her heart around the freedom that only God's love can bring.

I've worshiped God in many different places and in different ways, but some of my favorite moments of worship had a certain degree of love and freedom attached:

- I'm sitting in the floor of an apartment in Dallas at 3 A.M. Pages of new words are fanned out in front of me, and the song "Captivated" by Vicky Beeching is playing softly from my computer. The dream is out now; out of my heart and open before God. I'm praying over all of it and singing through the song, giving Him those words. With every part of my heart and imagination, I want to give this passion back as an offering to Him. I want Him to use it for His glory. I want to stretch out everything I write in this lifetime, every story, song, sonnet and poem, in one long love letter to my God. *Thank You, God, for creating expression and art, wild colors and words that dance through the halls of my imagination for hours on end.* Before the words were refined, fixed or even shared, they were His alone.

· Chase and I are driving along a high mountain road. The windows are down in his car. The sun is sinking into the high gray mountains and, as it fades, the sky seems to catch fire. Out the other window, on the opposite part of the sky, sits the moon. It is perfectly round and pale, a focal point for the coming stars. It strikes me as so beautiful, all this dark and light, this huge majesty and glory smashed together against one sky. I think of how the heavens declare the glory of God. The song "Mighty to Save" by United is playing loud through the speakers. I sing along and slip my hand out the window to let the moonlight push through my fingertips. *Thank You, God, for Your magnificent creation. I know I'm just one song rising toward the punched-tin sky. I can't imagine that my words mean more to You than a perfect sunset or a sky full of stars, but still You say I'm worth more to You than any of that.*

· I'm in Atlanta. I'm in a sea of college students and 20-somethings, and we all sing the songs on the screen and praise the God of our unknown futures. For those few minutes, the focus is off our exorbitant amount of student loan debt, off the crush we can't stop thinking about, and off all the pressure and the concern. The focus is just on Jesus. *God, I can rest easy because You're taking care of me. I can fall back into Your arms and know that You aren't closing Your eyes to this part of my life. Thank You for holding all the pieces of my life together in Your hands. Be glorified through this season.*

• I'm at a funeral listening to hundreds of people sing Matt Redman's "Blessed Be Your Name." *"You give and take away, but my heart will choose to say, 'Blessed be your name.'"* In that moment, we are living out our worship. We cry and question and wonder about God's timing, but we are wrapped in His love. We know the story doesn't end there. Even as we say goodbye for now, we allow our imaginations to picture a day when death dies away. *Thank You, Lord, for the promise of eternity. Thank You for holding me through the deep.*

• I'm standing on a beach in Miami, and I can feel my feet sinking into the sand. Lightning is caught in the far-off clouds. There are 20 of us standing there by the ocean, and as someone plays guitar, we sing songs about the God we love. We're ready to carry His name into the rainforests and the cities of a beautiful new continent. We're ready to rebuild an orphanage and kick soccer balls with kids in the streets and help wash hair at a community health fair. We are ready to carry love to this scary, wonderful new place. Something about this moment feels right. Our worship is about to move into action. The song is about to carry into how we live. *Thank You, God, for loving the whole world. Thank You for giving me a chance to carry Your love. Thank You for rejoicing over me with singing. I hope my life sings back to You.*

"A time is coming," Jesus told the woman by the well, "when you will worship the Father neither on this mountain nor in Jerusalem." By the well and by the ocean, from the mountains to cathedrals to the side of the beach, I want Him to teach me what it means to worship in spirit and truth. I want to be the kind of girl whose life sings in adoration and love for the one true God. I want my life to embody that picture I saw by the pier that day.

I want to worship God with the same reverent love those people had. I want to approach Him with abandon now when I'm 20-something and mostly confused but crazy enough to look at the world through eyes of compassion, idealism, hope and romance. I want to engage my culture with His love.

And I want to worship Him when I'm 50-something and probably still a little bit too idealistic but more refined somehow in the way I live and love. I want to be more intense about the way I'm pursuing Him and more mature in my faith, but I still want to approach life with a childlike heart.

And when my eyes are encased in wrinkles—when I can barely hold up my hands—I still want to worship Him from the center of my heart. I want Him to have all of me now, then and forever. I want to watch the waves crash against the sand and fall even more in love with the God who captured my heart at 9, and 19, and 90. I want to hear a familiar song and remember that morning by the pier when a praise chorus filled the sky and birdsong filled the air; when I saw people dancing and sailboats slipping across the water. I want to remember the little bursts of sunlight that made their way through moss trees; a patchwork of beautiful bright light, defiant against the darkness.

Enter the unquenchable worshipper. This world is full of fragile loves—love that abandons, love that fades, love that divorces, love that is self-seeking. But the unquenchable worshipper is different. From a heart so amazed by God and His wonders burns a love that will not be extinguished. It survives any situation and lives through any circumstance. It will not allow itself to be quenched, for that would heap insult on the love it lives in response to.

MATT REDMAN, FROM
THE UNQUENCHABLE WORSHIPPER[3]

Confessions

*Lord, when I catch a glimpse of Your love, Your kindness
and Your holiness, I don't want to log it in the back
corner of my mind as commonplace. I want to
live a life of worship. I want to love You with my whole heart.
I want to be a woman who worships You in
spirit and in truth. Thank You for giving me the
freedom to be real before You and to be genuine in
how I love You. In reverence and abandon and love, I want
to love You with all I am and all I'm becoming.*

Notes
1. Notes of John 4, *Integrity's iWorship Daily Devotional Bible* (Brentwood, TN: Integrity, 2003), p. 1389.
2. To read specific worship centered on God's holiness, see Psalm 29:2, Psalm 99:5 and Hebrews 12:28.
3. Matt Redman, *The Unquenchable Worshipper* (Ventura, CA: Regal, 2001), p. 18.

Love that Moves

*Then, leaving her water jar, the woman went back to the town
and said to the people, "Come, see a man who told me
everything I ever did. Could this be the Christ?" They came out
of the town and made their way toward Him.*

JOHN 4:28-30

❀ ❀ ❀

*If I speak with human eloquence and angelic ecstasy
but don't love, I'm nothing but the creaking of a rusty gate.
If I speak God's Word with power, revealing all his mysteries
and making everything plain as day, and if I have faith
that says to a mountain, "Jump," and it jumps, but I don't love,
I'm nothing. If I give everything I own to the poor and even
go to the stake to be burned as a martyr, but I don't love,
I've gotten nowhere. So, no matter what I say, what I believe,
and what I do, I'm bankrupt without love.*

1 CORINTHIANS 13:1-3, *THE MESSAGE*

❀ ❀ ❀

Her dress looked as if it were cut from diamonds.

It was fitted through the top and waist, and then it belled
into a long skirt that caught the light every time she moved.
When her name was announced, and Reese Witherspoon won
the Academy Award for playing June Carter Cash in *Walk the
Line*, she looked as if she'd stepped out of a fairytale into the
kind of reality every woman dreams of. I cheered from my living room. I'm a sucker for Cinderella moments.

We may not want to be recognized for our work in film. We
may not want sparkling dresses and heels. But I think most of

us are waiting for a moment when we "arrive." We dream about the moment when we look beautiful and accomplished; when we take center stage in the life we've always hoped for. And it wouldn't hurt if, in that moment, we're wearing a dress that looks like it's made of stardust.

The acceptance speech Witherspoon made that night was a three-minute burst of joy. Ever poised and elegant, she was still a little breathless and overwhelmed by it all. She clutched her golden trophy, looked out over a sea of faces with a sincerely surprised smile, and quoted her film character, June Cash: "I'm just trying to matter."

That resonated with me. Sitting in my living room, with a messy ponytail and wearing ripped jeans and a gray T-shirt, I was trying to matter, too. I was trying to figure out what (and who) I loved. I was trying to figure out where I belonged and what place might feel like "home" to me—what job was tailor-made for me to do. I wasn't hoping for an award or a gorgeous dress or six-inch heels (I would fall flat on my face in those), but I wanted to matter somehow, even if it was just to one person. I wanted one person to think I erred on the side of quirky instead of weird (it's a fine line, trust me). I wanted one person (besides my parents) to tell me I was beautiful. I wanted to know I was investing my time in issues that mattered. Give me a poster board and some markers and I'll rally and picket all day if it's something that moves me.

I wanted someone to validate the words I had spent hours molding, changing and scribbling into notebooks, the backs of receipts, and the back of my hand. I wanted to fast-forward my life 10 years, think back about that particular season, and know I didn't waste it. I didn't want to just take up space on this blurry blue planet. I wanted to matter while I'm here.

I was so inspired that I grabbed my Pringles can and stood up to give a speech. Then reality settled in: Underlying my burning passion to live a life that matters is the consciousness of what seems like a mile-long waiting list. I'm always waiting.

I think I'm on the cusp of figuring out something, putting this giant puzzle piece of my future in place, when someone reminds me that God's timing isn't like my timing. I feel like I am always waiting. I waited for high school to end and college to start. When my dreams of college life were dashed by dorms that persistently reeked of Ramen, I dreamed of graduating. I'm waiting for the right job (and cringe when I realize it's probably still years away).

Most of us are like that, don't you think? We're waiting to fall in love. We're waiting for the moment we set foot on foreign soil for the first time, or the day we see our book on a shelf, or the day we hold a baby in our arms. It's easy to wrap up life flat on a page like that—a long list of Cinderella moments somewhere out in the future, but never close enough to touch.

I'm guilty of believing that this moment in my life only connects me to some bright elusive moment in my future. I forget that life is only flat on a page for paperdolls. I forget what godly passion can accomplish in the world and that passion and compassion trump age and experience. The dreams and desires burning in my heart are there for a reason. I'm already in the story of my life. I'm not waiting to turn the page. I'm really living this. At some point, I've got to learn how to balance patience as God works in me with a passionate urgency to share His love with a hurting world.

Sam's story reminds me of that same concept in this part of her journey. She realized that today mattered; that this moment mattered. She would no longer just live through wasted days; she was ready to really *live*. She was ready to take a risk and be brave. Once Jesus' love became real to her, she couldn't sit still. She had to share it.

There's no red carpet rolled out in Samaria. Sam was clutching a water jar in her arms, not a trophy. But this was her Cinderella moment, too. The girl who had walked toward the well defeated, alone and broken was about to run back into the village full of excitement, compassion and freedom. She was about to carry a message of love that would change her world. She was about to prove that love—real unconditional love—changes everything. Even a paperdoll.

I AM

Let's focus in again on the scene by the well. By this point, we should be seeing the flicker of understanding in Sam's eyes as she talks to Jesus. She is piecing together who He is: more than a man, possibly more than even a prophet. We can only imagine the hope laced into the words as she speaks of the coming King: "The woman said, 'I know the Messiah will come—the one who is called Christ. When he comes, he will explain everything to us'" (John 4:25, *NLT*).

Remember, Jesus has very tactfully (but not rudely) made it clear that He knows everything about her. He knows what worship really is. He knows where living water really comes from. Jesus then wraps up His conversation with the Samaritan woman with a phrase that puts every acceptance speech to shame: "Then Jesus told her, 'I am the Messiah!'" (v. 26, *NLT*).

As Jesus is revealing His divinity to an ordinary woman from Samaria, the disciples come back on the scene. Surprised, and probably a little shocked, they say nothing at first. She didn't pause to gauge their reaction. She took the message back to Samaria.

All along, the love she was searching for was sitting right there in front of her. When she realized that this man was the Savior of the world, the revelation sent shockwaves to her paperdoll heart. She could have gone back into the village with a smug look on her face. She could have kept the result of that meeting a secret. After all, if the people in her town didn't care about her, why should she care about them?

In that split second, she made a choice that reverberated through history: she chose to share God's love with the world. She didn't let her age, her station in life or the fear of rejection hold her back. Her response is pretty wonderful:

The woman left her water jar beside the well and *ran* back to the village telling everyone, "Come and see a man who told me everything I ever did! Could he possibly be the Messiah?" So the people came streaming from the village to see him (John 4:28-30, *NLT,* emphasis added).

Sam, filled with the love of God, had a passionate urgency to go back to the village and share her story. There's no extreme makeover here (not externally, at least); no red carpet rolled out. She went back looking the same—but completely transformed inside. Suddenly, the opinions of her community didn't matter. Her worth was rooted in the Man by the well. This completely ordinary girl had a message to share with the world. And, in just the same way, God has also given us an opportunity to carry the message of His love, starting exactly where we are.

God's love gives us the ability to go back to a place of pain and make it a place of ministry as well. Let's set our eyes on Samaria and start walking.

Don't Get Too Comfy

Muffled under a growing pile of jeans and T-shirts, I heard my ringtone repeating. I scrambled out of the closet and started throwing clothes until I found it. The cute chirpy voice on the other end of the line immediately brought a smile to my face.

"Taylar!" I said, plopping down beside my open suitcase.

Taylar had been one of the campers in my cabin that summer, one of the girls who had actually made camp bearable. Her spunky sweetness rubbed off on the other campers. Despite the insane Texas heat, the flock of mosquitoes waiting to assault us everyday when we walked to breakfast, and various other not-so-fun caveats of camp life, nobody could stay in a bad mood around Taylar.

One aspect of Taylar's personality I particularly loved was her courage. At first glance, she didn't look like a risk-taker. She was the smallest girl at camp (possibly even shorter than me), with big gorgeous eyes and a smile that covered her face. She was very sweet and girly, but Taylar also seemed to like getting out of her comfort zone. She didn't let fear of the unknown hold her back. Instead, she let it propel her forward. I watched her flip across a stage to win a talent show, dancing like it was the last dance she would ever perform. She would move to physically wrap her arms around people and pray for them during the week. Some girls worried incessantly about fitting in. They only wanted to befriend the right people. Taylar wanted to befriend everybody. She seemed fearless.

A few days after we left mosquito land, Taylar started texting me about a dream in her heart that had started at camp but kept getting stronger: She wanted to lead a Bible study at the nursing home near her house. I assumed that when she said this was a "dream," she meant it was a distant dream—a far out future hope she had for someday. I thought leading a Bible study at the nursing home would be on Taylar's "when" list.

I was wrong. We were only a week past camp when I got the phone call.

After a very quick hello, Taylar jumped straight to the point of conversation.

"I was wondering if you could pray with me. Like right now?"

"Sure thing," I said. "What are we praying about?"

"I'm going to the nursing home. I start today. I'm walking there right now."

She said the activities coordinator seemed a little surprised when Taylar told her she was only 13. I was not surprised in the least. I pictured her walking toward the nursing home, her dark ponytail bouncing as she walked, and thought immediately of Paul's words to Timothy:

Don't let anyone look down on you because you are young, but set an example for the believers in speech, in life, in love, in faith and in purity (1 Tim. 4:12).

As I prayed with Taylar, I thought about all the dreams I've shelved. I decide I'll wait until I'm older . . . or more articulate . . . or less afraid. Too many silly excuses seem like legit reasons to ignore the passion God puts in my heart. But Taylar wasn't like that. She wanted to share the love of God *now*. She was afraid and unsure of what to expect, but she was determined to carry His love. And so she moved.

Taylar got what so many of us miss: Yes, God would use her someday to carry His love into the world and would work through her career and her life, but He was also using her *now*. She was setting an example *now*. She didn't allow the shabby excuse that she was too young to do something from God to prevent her from living life to the fullest, starting that second. She knew that this season in her life mattered. She was only 13 and didn't have years and years of Bible training under her belt. She wasn't even out of middle school. But what she did have was more important: she had a real, genuine relationship with God. And she wanted to share that love with other people.

She knew love matters most.

Love matters more than eloquence or age, more than physical ability or crazy circumstances. God uses normal, ordinary people to accomplish His work.

Just like Sam.

Just like us.

Picture the Samaritan woman walking back toward her community. Now picture the disciples standing there, mouths open, still a little dumbfounded at what just took place there. They urge Jesus to eat, but He quickly reminds them that there is something more important happening by the well than food. These are Jesus words to them:

> My food . . . is to do the will of him who sent me and to finish his work. Do you not say, "Four months more and then the harvest"? I tell you, open your eyes and look at the fields! They are ripe for harvest (John 4:34-35).

A whole field of opportunity is already open to us, too. We can't lose sight of what's important. We can't let comfort, or fear, keep us from sharing love with a world desperate to hear it.

Sam could have sat still. She didn't have to go back into her village. But if she'd chosen to keep that love to herself, she would have missed out on one of the most beautiful moments in history. When I see this part of her story, I can't help but wonder what I'm missing out on when I'm too afraid to carry his love into the world.

How Love Changed Samaria

As I was shopping for a new cell phone recently, I became enamored with a device that promised me constant connection to the world. On this one little phone, which also happened to be stylish and small (and pink), I could check my email, keep up with blogs and have unlimited texting. Occasionally I could even talk on the thing if I wanted. It seemed like such an exciting prospect: I would never be disconnected. I'm not tech-savvy, but the idea was appealing. Technology makes it possible for us to constantly be connected. At least that's what we think.

I am a mere phone call or text message away from friends ready to chat. I can email someone a note and know it will arrive in seconds. I can jump on a social networking site, see the status of all my "friends," and discover whether they're feeling focused or sad or excited. But if I embrace all that technology and don't really get to know people—know what they love, what makes them sad and what their passions are—I'm missing the real point of community.

The longer I looked at this dazzling new phone, the more I started to think about how many numbers in my current phone I don't even call anymore. I always wonder just how many of the 6 trillion "friends" people have on their Facebook are really people they *know*. It would seem pretty obvious that the world is longing to be part of a community.

The more technically connected we get, the more emotionally isolated we seem to become. We can work, carry on conversations, order dinner and watch a movie without ever getting off the couch. But no matter how we kid ourselves, we're still isolated if we're not actually spending face time with people. That's why I'm glad God didn't just send a letter to Sam. He didn't just send a messenger. He went there personally, made eye contact with her, and gave her the courage to go back into the community that didn't really care who she was. People need people. We're created to do life together.

This brings us to another important question: *What is our Samaria?* It's exactly where we are. It's the family, the campus and the community we are already part of. It may feel just as awkward and uncomfortable for us as it did for Sam, but God's love can give us the same courage to go back and make a difference there.

In looking at Sam's story, I thought of the following questions we could ask ourselves to determine if we are impacting the place where we already are:

- *Am I engaging my Samaria with forgiveness and grace?* The Samaritan woman didn't go back into town with a cruel attitude, listing the sins of all the people there. She didn't start talking about what was wrong with their lives. Instead, she simply said, "Come meet the man who knew everything I ever did." Love, not judgmental arrogance, is always what makes people take note and listen to what we have to say.

- *Am I serving people who can get me absolutely nowhere?* Real friendships should never be strategic. If we befriend people based on their social status, we're building a relationship on quicksand. Nothing about the people Jesus spent time with were a good move for Him politically. By all standards, He didn't align Himself with the prestigious crowd. Instead, He reached out to people who seemed to spend a lot of time on the fringe. We need to love that way. We need to make an effort to serve people who can give us nothing in return.

- *Am I carrying the love of God within my school?* School is busy and, quite possibly, eight hours of extreme boredom, but it is also teeming with opportunities to love genuinely.

- *Am I carrying the love of God into my family?* We didn't get to pick them, but we do have to live in the same house with them. No matter how big, or small, or unconventional your family is, there is probably a way to show God's love in what you do and say.

- *Do I care for the needs of others within my ministry environment?* Are we disguising prayer requests as gossip? Are we being intentional about making others feel welcome? Do we make an effort to include everyone in the conversation?

- *What is happening in my community?* What is the biggest social need facing the community? Is it poverty? Illiteracy? What could we do with our talents and time that could make a difference?

We can start in Samaria, where the fields are ripe for harvest. God has a work for us to do there.

How Love Changed the World

I had a paperdoll moment the other day. I was curled up in the rocking chair on my front porch reading a back issue of *National Geographic*. There was a gorgeous layout of Mount Vesuvius rising high above Naples, Italy. According to the article, when Vesuvius erupted thousands of years ago, the people of the nearby city of Pompeii didn't see the eruption coming and didn't have time to run. The entire city—along with the majority of its citizens—were buried under the ash.

Vesuvius is still active, darkening the sky over Naples like a sleeping dragon. I looked at pictures of chic Italians walking in the streets below, either oblivious to the danger that is constantly lurking above them or just impartial to it at this point. I'd heard of Pompeii, but I never connected all the pieces together. I never thought of how many people would be affected by a catastrophe like that. I had never seen the way the mountain looked so terrifying and beautiful against the sky. I was fascinated.

Under my *National Geographic* was a magazine I'd picked up because it promised to help me find the right jeans for my body type. The first eight pages show movie stars walking around and drinking coffee and eating chips and salsa. For some reason I really don't understand, that interests me. In fact, I could name every celebrity on the pages. But I didn't know that the name of the mountain that engulfed Pompeii thousands of years ago was called Vesuvius, or that it was still active.

I may know what the most recent celebrity couple is naming their kids, but I often forget that in the time it takes to type that sentence, a child starved to death in a ravaged African village. I have a way of limiting my scope of the world to only the things I want to see, and when I do that, I am missing out on a great and beautiful calling. When did I want to stop engaging culture with love? When did my world get so small?

I think one of Sam's most powerful lessons by the well was when she realized that the life she was living wasn't just about her. There were more needs out there than just her needs. There were other people in her village who were desperate for love. The same is true for our world: people are dying, desperate for food, water, education and hope. We aren't here just to smile pretty and take up space. We are here to impact that world.

What cause makes your heart skip a beat? What world issue gets you so fired up you feel like you can talk about it for hours? Maybe you get excited when you talk about building wells in communities with no clean water. Maybe the plight of illiteracy, which is still rampant even in our corner of the world, makes your heart skip a beat. Maybe child advocacy is where your heart lies: you're determined to make sure people know the truth about sex trafficking, child soldiers and the vast amount of orphans waiting for homes and hope.

From disability rights to the wars in the Sudan, from inner cities to African hillsides, poverty and injustice will hallmark our generation if we sit back and do nothing. But if we, like Sam, choose to walk into the world, we can change it. Our generation could be one marked by compassion, servanthood, advocacy and passion. Love is an incredible movement to be part of.

 "Our lives begin to end the day we become silent about things that matter." — Martin Luther King Jr.

So, what could you do today to show love to others and impact the world? Here are a few ideas:

- *Pray continuously for those in need.* Be specific in your prayers. Sometimes, I find that it helps if I pray for someone by name or for a particular family. Most organizations have ongoing email lists full of prayer prompters or updates.

- *Stay current on the needs of a people group close to your heart.* Look for articles about them in the news. Cut out pictures from magazines that remind you to pray for them. Familiarize yourself with websites and resources that keep you informed of their needs. Make your words count—write to your senators and congressmen thanking them for the work they are doing to meet these people's needs and encourage them to continue using their influence in ways that matter.

• *Put a picture of those in need where you can see it.* A friend sent me a picture that broke my heart. It was a picture of a child, starving, crawling hopelessly toward humanitarian aid miles away. In the background, a vulture sat, waiting. The bird had marked this child as its prey, and it seemed locked into following it until the child breathed its last breath. The picture is horrific and heartbreaking, but I keep it on my computer for days when I go paperdoll. That is the world I turn a blind eye to sometimes. And that is the world I cannot forget. Maybe you could put up a picture from a missions trip or even a piece of art or a quote that inspires you to keep fighting for someone else's rights.

• *Use your resources to make a difference.* Although my time is limited, I know I have far more of that to give than money. But even giving financial resources is sometimes more doable than I realize. I can't give away thousands of dollars, but I can drink one less cup of coffee each week and put that money toward something that matters. What if you were to save 10 bucks and send it out to a cause you support at the end of the month? Or have a can drive? What if you dragged your friends out of bed early one Saturday and built a ramp for a handicapped person through Habitat for Humanity? Whether you volunteer to make posters for Race for the Cure or get with your Bible study group and sponsor another little sister in Christ on the other side of the world, get creative in how you use your resources.

• *Prayerfully consider stepping out into the world yourself.*
Whenever I think of the way missions can impact lives,
I think of a girl named Laura. Laura was a vivacious red-
head who loved to read, laugh and spend time in worship. Laura and I met on a missions trip to Brazil. One
of the highlights of the trip for me was hearing how she
processed what she was experiencing. One day, her
team went to one of the Brazilian dumps, which was
teeming with men and women who lived there, and
sorted through trash. At the dump, two little girls attached themselves to Laura. They wanted to hang out
with her the whole day. They loved being carried and
picked up. They wanted to touch her red hair. At one
point, Laura sat down on a pile of trash and both little
girls jumped in her lap. Oblivious to the sounds, the
smells, and the trash, Laura realized the power of love.
She said that moment was a perfect metaphor of what
Jesus had done for her. He was willing to go through
the messy part of life with her. He was willing to go into
a broken world to win her back. He held her close,
oblivious to the junk in her life, and gave her this message to carry to the world. She didn't have a great deal
of money or a famous last name, but she knew she
could love. She wanted to love the way Jesus loved, both
there at the dump and for the rest of her life. I've never
forgotten Laura's story. Whenever you step out into the
world, do it with the intention to serve other people.
Without fail, God will minister to your heart as well. It's
amazing how genuine service leads to genuine love.

Away from the Well and Into the World

There are loads of reasons we stay put and don't move into
Samaria (or the world) to share the love of God. A few in particular come to mind:

Paperdolls Often Choose Apathy Over Advocacy

If we adopt the paperdoll mentality, we may have a tendency to sit around by our pity pools and compare tan lines. We reason the world is too big and the problems are too great to try and help. When we experience the fullness of God in our lives, however, passion begins to trump apathy every time. Sometimes the crisis seems too big and the problems too great, but filled with the courage of God, we go anyway. One girl can make a difference. Just ask Sam.

"There are many losing battles worth investing in, simply because winning is not the point." — Sarah Groves

Paperdolls Can Be Too Cavalier About Time

I've noticed that women of every age seem to have this unwritten competition: who leads the busiest life? It's the first thing we say when we call each other. "I'm so busy." Every time I work with high school students, I stand in awe at the way they fill up their calendars so fast. Between practice and studying and family time and church time, it's amazing they ever sleep.

I'm learning that life only gets busier.

I'm not saying it's a bad thing to be busy. In fact, I get bored if I'm not doing something. But I think sometimes I'm guilty of filling up my calendar and thinking all those appointments and plans makes my life matter more. I've been so busy doing church stuff I let my personal time with the Lord slide. I've been through busy seasons where I've neglected dear friends. The truth is, I will make time for what I love. And an even more somber truth is this one: I really don't have all the time in the world.

Only God knows the number of days we have on this planet. For us, the amount of time we have remains a mystery. And that's why time is one of the most precious gifts we can give.

Paperdolls Sometimes Value Comfort Above All Else

I remember reading a story about Elisabeth Eliot, a missionary to the Huaorani tribe in Ecuador. After the tribe her family had tried to serve killed her husband, Jim, she was afraid to return. Who wouldn't be? In fact, I'm fairly certain I would never, ever want to go back. However, like the Samaritan woman, Elisabeth trusted God to make her place of pain a place of ministry for her.

At first, Elisabeth wanted to wait to return until the fear had subsided. But it never subsided; it was always there, gnawing at her heart and stomach. Finally, a friend gave her a brilliant piece of advice: *Do it afraid.* If she had let fear hold her back from that opportunity, she would have missed something tremendous: Elisabeth was able to see the men who had killed her husband give their lives to Jesus Christ.

Elisabeth's ministry still touches thousands. She engaged life head on with butterflies in her stomach. Whether it's fear of the unknown, fear of rejection, or just fear, we need to learn to lean on God. He's bigger than our biggest fear.

Becoming Love

One time, Jesus went to His hometown and talked about what His mission was on earth. He quoted Isaiah 61:1-2, saying:

> The Spirit of the Lord is on me, because he has anointed me to preach good news to the poor. He has sent me to proclaim freedom for the prisoners and recovery of sight for the blind, to release the oppressed, to proclaim the year of the Lord's favor (Luke 4:18-19).

Jesus was passionate about reaching the poor, the imprisoned, the blind and the oppressed. I want to get wrapped up in a love that looks like that.

We will carry some kind of message to the world, be it one of consumerism and false happiness or the extraordinary love of God. In our paperdoll moments, that message can sound flashy and fake, more like a "clanging cymbal," as Paul would say. But when we use our voices to champion the needs of the people around us, we become God's love song to the world. No more loud commercials. No more clanging cymbals. No more broken record.

Sam's story ends—and a new chapter in her life begins—with a specific and unusual sound. She doesn't get applause for the change in her life. We don't hear a team cheering her on as she goes back into the village. Instead, we hear the sound of empty water jars hitting the ground. Nothing compares to knowing Jesus. No water compares to living water.

We hear other sounds, too: her breath as she rushes back into Samaria, and her voice as she talks about the man who knew everything she had ever done. She doesn't have to be ashamed, because He wasn't ashamed of her. She can speak with confidence, because He is confident in her. If we'd been in Samaria, I think we would have heard a bold passion in her voice that day.

And then we hear the murmurs and footsteps of an entire village walking up toward the well. I'm willing to bet they'd all been to the well too—maybe not the physical one to draw water, but definitely a well of dissatisfaction. I think they were just as eager to figure out what living water was all about. Paper gets so boring after a while. Real life is so much more appealing. I'm glad Sam was willing to share her story.

Sam's place of pain became a place of ministry. What if we allowed God's love to give us the same courage to move into the world with forgiveness and grace? What if instead of spending our lives stacking success after success, trying to prove something to someone who hurt us in the past (or just to prove it to ourselves), we let love heal those broken places? We don't have to be ashamed. We can walk in confidence, because He is confident in us.

This moment matters. This season isn't just a bridge from one point to another. We shouldn't get so fixated on five years down the road that we miss the work God has for us today. This season is for something, for someone besides just ourselves. Love, at its best, doesn't fester in our hearts. It moves us out into the world.

I don't want to live a life full of clanging cymbals and gongs and broken glass. Instead, I want to live a life that sings.

True love frees us up. Love lets us worship the way we want. Love gives us permission to dance to our own music and sing songs we make up out of thin air. Love doesn't care if our jeans are from Target or Saks. Love isn't into labels. Love looks past a fake smile and into an aching heart. Love forgives.

Love isn't obsessed with celebrity; it pushes another person into the spotlight instead. Love is the first to give a round of applause. Love uses 15 minutes of fame to make an impact that will last a lifetime. Love sees something more important than bad hair days, designer bags and pop culture. Love is counterculture, fighting the good fight even when losing is imminent Love sees a world that is dying, empty, alone and afraid and offers hope and acceptance. Love doesn't back down. Love vows to change the world. It pushes past emotion or feeling to the act of doing. Love is a voice for the voiceless. Love is a light in the darkness. Love is the advocate, the rebel, the dreamer the world is waiting for. And love doesn't just dream—love moves.

So be that girl. Be that girl who can love outrageously, because she is loved unconditionally.

Confessions

*Lord, take every apathetic whimper and make it a brave
new song. Show me how to use my time, energy and
passion in a way that will directly touch another person's life.
Give me courage to move into the world—even if I am afraid—
and help me to become a moving, breathing example of the
love You've poured over my life.*

Note

1. Translated directly from the Greek, Jesus' words by the well become even more beautiful to us: "I am, the one speaking to you." Jesus directly links Himself with the God of the Old Testament (Exodus 3:14 reads, "God replied to Moses, 'I AM WHO I AM. Say this to the people of Israel: I AM has sent me to you'").

10

Paper Violets

*And I kept wondering about the people who met Christ who were
losers in the lifeboat, the crippled and the blind, the woman at the well,
Mary Magdalene and Zacchaeus. Entire communities had shunned
them and told them they were no good, but God, the King of the Universe,
comes walking down the street and looks them in the eye, holds their
hands, embraces them, eats at their tables, entered their homes for
all to see. That must have been the greatest moment of their lives.*

DONALD MILLER, FROM
SEARCHING FOR GOD KNOWS WHAT[1]

*Many of the Samaritans from that town believed in him because
of the woman's testimony. . . . They said to the woman, "We no longer
believe just because of what you said; now we have heard for ourselves,
and we know that this man really is the Savior of the world."*

JOHN 4:39,42

London was always ready to surprise me with a random slice of
history. It seemed as if every piece of architecture in that city,
from a specific red door to a run-down pub, had a fabulous
story attached to it. One particular discovery that took me by
surprise was Alfred Hitchcock's name engraved into a building
fairly close to the flat my friends and I stayed in. He had lived
in that building at one time, or so the sign read. We stared at
his name for a while, thinking it might make us cool by osmo-
sis, and wondered if the street we lived on had inspired one of
his strange stories.

Suddenly, the names of famous people kept cropping up
everywhere, like four leaf clovers in our urban kingdom. Many

buildings had names carved on them of famous residents who had lived there at one time: authors, poets, playwrights and directors. The roads and parks were full of ornate monuments dedicated to great kings and queens and world leaders—men and women who have passed on but managed to leave quite a legacy behind. London knows how to celebrate history, especially the people who made history sizzle.

It seemed like the bigger the monument, the more "important" the person was. And yet, the coolest monument in London (in my humble opinion) is actually easy to miss. It belongs to Sir Christopher Wren, a brilliant architect who redesigned London after the great fire of 1666. Where most people saw hopelessness after such a tragedy—a future as dark as the smoke rising to the sky—Wren saw hope. He saw beauty in the ashes and dared to imagine spires and buildings blooming from the rubble. One of his most famous works was St. Paul's Cathedral, an immaculate church with a rich history. When I stood beneath it and stared up at the spires scraping the rare blue sky, I couldn't help but marvel at its beauty.

I wasn't surprised to find out that Wren was buried in this building that had occupied so much of his heart, time and energy for years. What did surprise me was the lack of pomp surrounding his grave. The man had rebuilt the city, for crying out loud. You would think his grave would be surrounded with statues and monuments listing his achievements. But his tomb is quite simple, bearing only his name and his world-famous epitaph: "Underneath lies buried Christopher Wren, the builder of this church and city; who lived beyond the age of ninety years not for himself, but for the public good. Reader, if you seek his monument, look around you . . ."

Wren's laborious nights of dreaming and design—nights when hope and frustration burned in equal measure—now define the skyline of London. He didn't need a monument; his life's work *was* his monument. Wren was living for something greater than his own fame. It doesn't matter that his name probably doesn't register in our minds when we first hear it. His life's work outlasted his lifetime. His "monument" should remind us that a full life isn't measured in what we own or what family we come from or what town we're born in. True success is measured by how we live. It's not so much whether or not our name makes its way through history, but whether or not we leave a legacy behind that matters.

I've come to a conclusion. I believe that life is, in part, about Who I know, but not in the classic understanding of the phrase. The prophet Isaiah said it perfectly: "LORD, we show our trust in you by obeying your laws; our heart's desire is to *glorify your name*" (Isa. 26:8, emphasis added). Paperdolls seem to be bent on finding some version of status and fame, and I wonder if that craving for notoriety really comes from our heart's desire to leave a legacy that matters. I think maybe all this trying to make a name for ourselves leads us to the well time and time again because our focus is a bit off. We think some measure of celebrity will bring with it some measure of happiness. And it does bring happiness, I suppose, but fame in and of itself never brings fullness. There is another Name I'm living for; another Name I want to carry into the world. I want love to become my legacy.

That's why Sam's story could not be more applicable. Her name will remain a mystery. But we get to see the impact of her life. Her culture was changed by the message she carried, and her legacy continues to inspire thousands of people.

One last time, let's go back to Samaria to see the impact her life made.

When the Girl by the Well Met the Savior of the World

We've seen Sam running back toward her village, ready to bring folks back to meet the Man at the well. Picture the surprised look in a villager's eye as she runs past or the people that must have gathered around when she said she had something to say.

John tells us her message to the village was brief and to the point:

> The woman went back to the town and said to the people, "Come, see a man who told me everything I ever did. Could this be the Christ?" They came out of the town and made their way toward him (John 4:28-30).

They were moving all together now, back toward the well Sam just came from, burning with curiosity as to whether or not this man really was the Messiah. We're told that Jesus spent two more days with the Samaritan people and that when the people heard His words, many of them became just as eager for living water as the Samaritan woman.

> Many of the Samaritans from that town believed in him because of the woman's testimony, "He told me everything I ever did." So when the Samaritans came to him, they urged him to stay with them, and he stayed two days. And because of his words many became believers (John 4:39-41).

We couldn't ask for a more beautiful and fitting end to our time with the Samaritan woman than this last glimpse into her life:

> They said to the woman, "We no longer believe just because of what you said; now we have heard for ourselves, and we know that this man really is the Savior of the world" (John 4:42).

When an ordinary girl by a well met up with the Savior of the world, her life and her culture changed. The Samaritan woman's legacy didn't have to be a life of sin, a string of broken hearts, or a list of bad decisions. *Her legacy became one of love.* She may have risked more rejection or humiliation by walking back into her community, but she did it anyway. The personal impact that Jesus had made on her life showed. And because of her witness, lives were changed.

There's no building in Sychar with her name on it. We don't even know her name. But I don't think she would mind. I don't think making a name for herself was her ultimate goal. She just wanted her community to experience the living water she had found. She wanted them to know the Man who had changed her life. What a picture that must have been of an entire community streaming through the hills toward Jesus to share His love, and all because one woman was brave enough to return to the town that rejected her. What was true of London's great architect is also true of an ordinary Samaritan girl: *If you seek her monument, look around you.*

Living a Legacy

I have a feeling the Samaritan woman never walked back to the well the same way. I wonder if she went to the well when she heard news of the crucifixion and resurrection that took place later, celebrating and grieving all at the same time.

I wonder if she took her grandkids to Jacob's Well and told them about Jesus. I wonder if the women in the village talked about it, and thought about it, every time they drew water.

I keep imagining her walking back toward the well as an old woman, with soft white hair falling down over her shoulders. I wonder if she touched it with a shaky hand, closed her eyes and pictured His face. Maybe she even dreamed of the day she would close her eyes and be reunited with Him.

We can imagine many things that might have happened to her later, but I have a feeling that her time with Jesus by Jacob's Well was at the forefront of her mind for the rest of her life. I doubt anyone in Samaria ever looked at the well the same way again. The well would be a permanent symbol of the day many people came to know Jesus and of the day He spoke to the woman alone and gave her a message to share with the world. But the well was not her legacy. Love was her legacy.

Her words didn't just echo through Samaria after all; her words echo in the corners of our hearts half a world away. The story of the Samaritan woman in the Word of God has inspired thousands of scholars, writers, artists and teachers throughout the centuries. Her rally cry to Samaria wasn't a speech inciting her great life achievements; it was a simple call to come meet the Messiah. Her life became about His Name, not her own.

Based on her example and what I've read of her conversation with Jesus, I know I want to leave a godly legacy, too—starting *now*. As I thought about this, I noted some ways (although the list is endless) that my life could reflect His love:

- *I can be a girl who takes advantage of my time alone with the Lord, building a vibrant prayer life, getting rooted in His unchanging Word.* My paperdoll culture offers me many alternate versions of "truth": true beauty, true love, true purpose. I want to be in God's Word enough to know what He says. I want His Word, not my society's changing standards, to define me. I want to get wrapped up in the mystery of prayer and take advantage of my time alone with God. I have the same access to Him as the Samaritan woman did. I can run to the Man by the well, who sees my deepest needs and fills my soul to overflowing. I want to really know Him, not just know a little bit about Him.

- *I can live out a different definition of beauty in my life.* I've seen the pursuit of beauty break my heart. I've seen it wreck lives and cause deep pain. I'm old enough to know that broken hearts hide behind beautiful smiles. I don't want to think of beauty as a jean size anymore, or as the perfectly proportioned face of my favorite actress. I want to think of beauty as the radiant love of God inside me that flows outward. I want to bear His image with reverence and grace.

- *I can stand strong in His mercy and forgiveness, knowing He has covered all my sins.* It is fully possible to be 16, or 26, or 36—"young" by all practical standards—and still have parts of our past we would do anything to forget and erase. As true repentance becomes our hearts' cry and we turn away from sin, we also need to walk in His forgiveness. We don't have to keep reliving the mistake in our minds. We can rest in the confidence that our past doesn't define our future. In the same manner, because I have been forgiven, I want to be forgiving toward other people in my life.

- *I can strive for authenticity in my relationship with God.* When the time comes to celebrate, I want to celebrate big. When heartbreak comes, I'm walking through that with Him, too. I want to grieve loud and long. I want to laugh hard. I'm not a paper girl without emotions who thrives on autopilot, disconnecting herself from an aching world. I want to love God with my heart, mind, soul and strength. I know He's big enough for my questions; I know I don't even have to have all the answers. I don't want to be judgmental and mean. Instead, I want the way I live to honor God. I get to bring the world my most real, most creative self. The world may be full of fake, but I'm nobody's paperdoll. I want what I do and say to be genuine.

- *I can reach into my community—physically—and put my time, heart, and creativity into causes that stir my heart.* When it came to sharing the love of Christ, the Samaritan woman started right in her hometown. I want to do the same. I may not have a great deal of money or resources, but I can at least give my time.

• *I can broaden my understanding of the world and seek to impact that world with love and service.* My comfort level no longer limits the scope of my worldview. I want to get out of my culture. I want to be aware of what is happening in the world and see how my dreams, talents and creativity can help make it better.

• *I can search out people in their loneliness.* Because I know what it feels like to be left out, I want to make it a point to search out people and befriend them.

• *I can live a life of true, intimate worship.* Whether I'm alone or with other believers—in my car, in my job, in my life or anywhere else—I want my worship going to the only One who truly deserves it.

• *I can show evidence of God's love in my relationships.* I want to look for ways to serve my friends and family and acknowledge what they do for me. Even in broken families, the love of God can help us approach relationships with forgiveness and grace.

• *I can trust God's timing and leadership in all my romantic relationships.* I am committed to saving my heart, and my body, for one man who loves God with all his heart and who loves and respects me as God says that he should. I know my heart's desires are safe in God's hands. I know He holds me through seasons of rejection. I want to wait, and anticipate, with joy.

• *I can get over myself and get out into a community, and a world, that may be stuck beside the well.* And I'll talk about the Man who knew everything I ever did—and loved me anyway.

My name doesn't matter. "It's written on water," as John Keats says. It's a blurb in the phone book. But His name matters; it matters in how I live every day. What I do as a career, or where I go, isn't the issue as much as how I glorify Him through what I do. I doubt I'll leave a legacy as a great world leader, an edgy artist or a music icon. But I can leave the legacy of a girl who loved deeply.

And that sounds like quite an amazing lifetime.

Paper Violets

Whenever I think about women who've left beautiful legacies, I think of my grandmother.

I thought of her the other day when I was walking to the grocery store. I saw a bouquet of the reddest roses I have ever seen; a true, perfect, unforgettable red like the perfect shade of lipstick. The petals felt like velvet paper, and when I touched them, I remembered the last conversation I had with her before she passed away.

I sat on the edge of her hospital bed that day holding a bunch of paper flowers; tangible proof of a season in my life underscored by confusion, frustration and panic attacks. I told a friend of mine I was fairly certain I was going crazy. She told me I should take up painting. Painters can get away with crazy. Late at night when I couldn't sleep, I turned on some music and smashed together pinks, reds, yellows and blues on a paper plate. Then I loaded that mess of color onto a brush and watched it bloom into flowers on a canvas, on paper, on plastic cups and on Mason jars. I painted anything I could get my hands on. I thought it might be fun to show my grandmother this new hobby, because she'd always appreciated my artsy side. When I spilled the paper flowers out of my pocket and onto my grandmother's bed, I suddenly felt very immature. But she thought they were adorable.

She asked me how I was doing. I lied and told her that I was so happy and excited about my future and that I was brimming with great stories and beautiful words. None of that was accurate. I was painting flowers at 2 A.M. and having strange breathless moments when I was around crowds of people. I was afraid of shadows and of being alone. Sometimes I cried through my prayers. Sometimes I didn't pray at all. The job I dreamed about didn't happen, and neither did the guy, and I couldn't write anything. It was as if all the words in the world had shriveled up and blown out of my imagination. And I knew I was about to lose her. I was having an awful time wrapping my mind around goodbye.

I stopped talking then, and my lip started to tremble. "Things aren't working out like I thought they would," I managed to whisper. I felt selfish as soon as the words left my mouth. I knew that moment of clarity could be our last conversation, and all I did was talk about my silly problems. She reached over and put her hand on my leg and smiled at me. When my eyes locked on hers, there was no fear there, only the confidence and grace I'd come to know so well.

"Everything works out for you," she said. "You're going to have to trust God in this. Keep moving ahead. He's always taken good care of you. He will always take good care of you. Hang on tight and watch and see."

I put my hand over hers. Her hand had wrinkles and bumps, but her skin felt like rose petals, dozens and dozens of them. I thought of how strange that picture must look. I was the young idealistic girl with her whole life ahead of her. I was supposed to be excited about the future, but I looked terrified. Gran was just inches from eternity. She should have been scared, but she looked so peaceful in that moment, so confident that the God who had carried her this far would carry her home.

"Love you," I whispered as a single cold tear rushed down my face.

"Love you more," she said as she squeezed my hand tight in hers.

That was our last conversation, the last stolen moment of mental alertness I had with her. Our story together ended with "I love you," her hand in mine and paper violets scattered on the white sheet between us. I thought about all the flowers and babies she'd held in her lifetime, about the dough she kneaded and the green beans she had snapped and the hands she had held in fierce, unrefined prayers that rattled the skies. Life is dying, too, and, in that, truly living. It's living every moment with deep intention, right up until we dance—or walk—or limp—that last glorious mile home.

And really, how we live is the point of it all. I want to live in the dailyness of my life, not just my daydreams. I want to keep moving through my fear, not back down because of it. I want to celebrate beauty and see it for what it really is and maybe even become something kind of like it. I don't want to get so caught up in becoming some cookie-cutter paper pretty that I miss beauty at its best—the kind that comes with a crooked smile, a song sang off key, a leftover ink stain from a night full of words. I never want to get so wrapped up in a TV character, or a girl in a book, that I only live in my imagination. Life isn't lived flat on a screen or flat on a page. Life is lived in breath and movement and cold air in my lungs, in the jagged line of the horizon and in the warm swirling hope that radiates from limb to limb when I know I have loved . . . and that I am loved. Real life is the presence of another person close to me, the weight of a hand covering mine, the weight of a soft kiss, the weight of my nephew sitting in my lap while we read another story before bed. It's the weight, and the risk, of saying "I love you" and meaning what I say.

Everybody talks about the big moments: weddings, babies, success, promotions and graduation days. But life isn't just lived in a handful of major events. Life is lived on fishing docks and at sewing machines, in front of a canvas, and in the melody of a worship song. For me, life is devoting myself to standing up for people who can't (or won't) stand up for themselves. It's all about fighting battles (even losing battles) and never getting recognized for it, and then going to bed exhausted but excited. Life is devoting myself to good art. It's cheap tacos with friends on Monday night, breakups, breakouts, phone calls, coffee so hot it burns my tongue, and movies so good I want to stand up and clap in the theater. Life feels like the verge of joy: like a guitar strap around my shoulders, a first awkward dance, the last line of a play, a laugh so loud and so hard I laugh too, even if I don't get the joke. It's a body breaking the surface of the water at a baptism and a baby yawning and stretching in the morning sunlight.

Life is knowing Jesus, inasmuch as my fragile human mind and heart can know Him. I don't understand His ways. He confuses me and inspires me. But I want Him more than anything.

I have been to a place where I wanted to fold into my paper smile and stop. I know the motions by now. I know the right things to say. It would be so easy to be a paperdoll. But more than wanting to look like my life is all together, I want to have what my grandmother had: a deep-rooted love for God that flows into my life. Life is messy and full of heartbreaking tragedies I never see coming until they envelop me. But somehow, love keeps me moving through all of that.

Sometimes I hear people say that their lives are boring. I'm guilty of thinking it, too. I start to think all these isolated moments of beauty don't matter, but they do. This season matters. I forget the stars above me are miracles, spoken out of God's breath into a fiery blue atmosphere. I forget the ground beneath me is a miracle, spoken out of God's breath into dirt, grass, roses and apple trees. And I forget the beating heart in my chest is a miracle, made with God's hands, created in His image. I want to live out that miracle, and live it well, right up until the end. As long as I have breath in me, I want to use it to love well.

I want to come to that end, and that beginning, and remember the richness of life I held in my lifetime. I want to have all my memories scattered around like paper flowers in my lap.

I want to have a thousand pictures running through my mind of the people I loved and the people who loved me. And I want to hold all that love like confetti in my hands and toss it in the air when I cross the finish line home.

Gran was right. God has never once let go of me. She knew, because she lived out that truth in her life. And just like my fabulous grandmother, just like the woman by the well, and just like so many beautiful women who've walked this path before, I'm determined to carry His love with me forever. I've tasted living water. I've known what it's like to walk in the fullness of God's love. Nothing else satisfies.

Last Glances

I have a feeling that this won't be the end of our journey with the Samaritan woman. Even though we're closing the book on her story now, I think it will resonate in all-new ways in our lives as we stumble into new seasons. Her story will touch our hearts 10, 20 and even 40 years from now in entirely different ways.

In the not so distant future, I hope her story will get caught in our hearts again. I hope we'll see something that will make us think of her story—water, a wishing well, a book full of beautiful paperdolls—and we'll flip back to John 4 just to read our favorite lines again, just to imagine the inflection in her voice, in His voice, when this glorious scene takes place.

From this point on, let's choose to live our stories. We're free from paperdoll standards. We can emulate a whole new kind of beauty. We aren't chained to artificial saviors anymore. We know who the Messiah is, and we can know Him personally.

This is the part where we get to choose to keep His love bottled up or share it with the world. This is where we get to take a risk and leap with no safety net in sight. Let's stop waiting for "somedays" and "what ifs." Let's drop the jars and run into the village and let love be the message we sing from the deepest parts of our paper hearts.

I saw a great quote that I think serves us well here at the end of our journey: "Look at the past. Don't stare at it." Bearing that advice in mind, let's picture the well one last time.

No one is there now. No shadows fall. Once that well had represented a point of pain for the Samaritan woman and had symbolized all the ways she'd gone looking for love in the wrong places. For the rest of her life, the well could have reminded her of her sin, her pain or her broken heart. But instead, it stood as a reminder of the Savior who met her right there on an ordinary day to set her free. It became a symbol of hope; part of the story of a girl who dared to dream great dreams and do great things for her God. She may have walked to the well defeated, but she walked back into the world transformed. *If you seek her monument, look around you.*

With that, we walk boldly into our stories, determined to leave our own legacies of love behind us. Filled with the love of Christ, who knows everything we've ever done and loves us anyway, we have a great message to carry this day: there is Someone waiting by the well who knows everything we ever did and loves us anyway.

You are nobody's paperdoll.

Walk confidently. Live with compassion. This season isn't just for you, so take big risks. Do great things. He's there to catch you when you leap. Lose yourself in the downpour of His extraordinary love. He has always been faithful to you. He will always be faithful to you. Taste and see that the Lord is good.

And thirst no more.

Note

1. Donald Miller, *Searching for God Knows What* (Nashville, TN: Thomas Nelson, 2004), p. 129.

Study Guide

This study guide is included as a prompter for taking some of the themes in the book deeper, but remember that these are merely suggestions. Don't feel limited to answering just the questions you see here. You're free to engage the text with your own creativity (really—the last thing this study guide should feel like is homework you struggle through!). Hopefully, you'll find plenty of suggestions here for further thought and study. Whether you try some of them, or all of them, is up to you. Make this story, and this book, your own.

Chapter 1
When Paper Hearts Come Alive

Soundtrack
"From the Inside Out," by Kristian Stanfill
"This Is Your Life," by Switchfoot

Questions
1. Take a look at some of the current magazines on the newsstand and think about the most prominent headlines. What do they seem to revolve around? Weight loss? Romance? How do you keep perspective on those issues? How does something move from healthy interest to obsession?

2. Have you ever gone through a season when "paperdolls" influenced too much of your thinking? What message did you (wrongly) believe to be true?

3. Remember that the point of Jesus' time on earth was never to condemn but to set free. If you were walking to Jacob's Well today, what do you think Jesus would talk to you about? What would you want to ask Him?

4. How do you engage God during "the ordinary"? Pause to think of three ways you've seen His work in your life today.

Further Reflection

Take some time to evaluate your own time alone with God. Does it feel intimate or stagnant to you? You might want to ask another female (maybe your mom, your mentor or your Bible study leader) what her time with God looks like to get some ideas for how to change around your own. Be specific in the questions you ask her. How does she pray? What does she do when her time with God feels stagnant? How does she study the Bible? Your time with God won't be the same as hers, but maybe you can get some new ideas for changing up the routine.

Further Text

Take some time to see what Jesus' ministry was like just before He met the woman by the well. Take a look at John 1-4. What was the public opinion of Jesus at this point? What were His disciples doing?

Chapter 2
Love Like Water and Chaos

Soundtrack

"Paper Doll," by Rosie Thomas
"For the Times When I Feel Faint," by Relient K

Questions

1. Using the examples given in this chapter (or maybe some we didn't even look at), what is your deepest "well" at this point in your life? Is there one well you go to looking for perfect love more than any other? Is there a well you think our culture pulls from more than another?

2. Have you ever been the odd girl out, like the Samaritan woman? What are some ways you can be a better friend to

the girls in your life? How do you stomp out gossip in your circle of friends?

3. Who are the "Samaritans" in your school and society? Is there a group that seems to be pushed aside (or made fun of) more than another? Is there a group people try to avoid? How can you help those people know the love of God?

Further Text
Read Psalm 103:3-5.

Chapter 3
Beautiful Scars

Soundtrack
"Mirror," by Barlow Girl
"Heal the Wound," by Point of Grace
"Inside Out," by April McLean

Questions
1. Take a look back at the "Beauty Redefined" section on pages 66-68. Think about the most beautiful women you know. What makes them that way? If you're doing this study in a small group, take some time to describe one of those women. Or take some time as a group to discuss what you think a biblical perspective of "beauty" really looks like. Now describe what kind of beautiful (physically, mentally, spiritually, emotionally) you want to be.

2. Where do you think all this insecurity comes from in our hearts? If we know we are who God says we are, why is it so hard for us to see ourselves that way?

3. Most of us are likely to pick out things about our bodies and personalities we don't like. Make a list of 10 things

about your body and 10 things about you that you think are pretty incredible. If you're doing this study with a friend, you may want to do this for each other.

Further Reflection

Despite occupying such a short passage in the Bible, the Samaritan woman's story has managed to make its way into various art forms over the decades. There are hundreds of paintings inspired by the Samaritan woman, but here are a few you might want to check out to start: Martorell's *Christ and the Samaritan Woman at Jacob's Well*, Louis Glanzman's *Samaritan Woman*, or (my personal favorite) Deeann Carson's *The Samaritan Woman*. Why do you think those artists chose to paint her the way they did? How do *you* picture her face? What's the strongest emotion you imagine radiating from her eyes? Is it surprise, shame, guilt, curiosity, hope or something entirely different? If you were an artist, what specific moment by the well would you try to capture in a painting? (If you are an artist, give it a shot!)

Further Text

What God says in His Word is absolute truth. So whatever our culture says about you that doesn't match up with God's Word is a lie. In navigating paperdoll culture, I've learned to do something that may seem kind of corny. But I hope you'll give it a try.☺ Take a verse of Scripture that talks about your worth in Christ, and then personalize it. For instance, for Psalm 45:11, you could say, "The King is enthralled by my beauty. I'm choosing to honor Him, because He is my Lord." Whenever you start down the all-too-familiar road of self-loathing, *say that verse out loud.* Something about hearing the truth of God's Word hit the air helps it sink into our hearts faster. For other examples of who you are in Christ, take a look at these verses: Ephesians 1:3-5; 1:7; John 8:31-32; 1 Thessalonians 1:4; 2 Corinthians 1:8-9.

Chapter 4
Waiting for Gilbert

Soundtrack
"For My Love," by Bethany Dillon
"Love Song for a Savior," by Jars of Clay

Questions

1. Who holds you accountable in the relationships you have with guys? If you don't have someone yet, pray for a friend or mentor who might. Write her initials in the margins. Make sure she's someone you can be completely honest and up front with about the emotional and physical boundaries you set.

2. Think about your favorite movie or love story. What's the name of the hero? What makes him so endearing in your eyes? Do you think Hollywood paints an accurate portrayal of what guys should be like? What are some biblical qualities we're told to seek out in our relationships?

3. Think about the concept of monkey's paw prayer. Are you ever afraid to share your deepest heart's desire with God? Are you afraid He'll withhold good from you just because He can? Take some time to pour out your heart, either verbally or on paper, alone before God.

4. Take inventory of the following areas of your heart when it comes to guys and relationships:

   Physical: Are you being conscious of your body language around guys? What boundaries do you have and how do you keep them in place? Who keeps you accountable in your decision?

Mental: What are you watching, reading, listening to or looking at that's making it harder to keep physical boundaries intact? How do you keep your mind pure when you live in a culture consumed by graphic media?

Emotional: Are you guarding your emotional attachment to the guys in your life? I've noticed, especially with college girls (and this was certainly an issue for me in college, too) that some of the most painful heartbreaks don't come from giving away too much of our bodies but our hearts. When the emotional connection we form with a guy severs—when we realize we're falling in love with him but he just wants to be friends—the rejection can be just as painful as a breakup.

Spiritual: Are you looking to God as your ultimate source of worth, or are you becoming somebody's paperdoll, trying desperately to be what you think he wants? Can the men in your life see God in you? Do they see your love for the Lord in the way you live?

Further Reflection

Take some time to pray about, and for, the guy who will one day steal your heart. You may even want to write a letter (even though you don't know his name) affirming the commitment that you've made this day to him, to yourself and to your God. Why are you waiting for him? What are the inner qualities that you hope he possesses? What are your hopes for your future together?

Further Text

Read 1 Corinthians 13:1-13. For an excellent read on maintaining emotional and physical purity, check out *Eyes Wide Open* by Brienne Murk and *Every Young Woman's Battle* by Shannon Ethridge.

Chapter 5
Dear Veruca Salt

Soundtrack
"You Are All I Need," by Bethany Dillon
"More than Enough," by Jeremy Camp

Questions

1. What is the most ridiculous extravagance you've seen? What is society's latest version of Veruca's golden egg?

2. Can you think of something you wanted (maybe even a toy when you were little) that you thought you had to have, but that proved to be a letdown in the end?

3. Make your own "Atlanta list." Off the cuff and without trying to be eloquent, what are you thankful for today? Think about the relationships you love. Think about specific attributes the people in your life possess. Think about your quirky favorites: your favorite smell, favorite emotion, favorite piece of art, favorite song. Be specific. What about your life, right now, are you thankful for?

Further Text
Read Matthew 6:2-4 and 6:19-24.

Chapter 6
Some Place Sudden, Dark and Deep

Soundtrack
"You Never Let Go," by Matt Redman
"Shadowfeet," by Brooke Frazier

Questions

1. Take some time today to share your deepest place of pain. First, write that experience out on paper, and then consider

sharing it with someone else. Now look at Jesus' prayer in John 17. If you're in a small group, have someone read aloud verses 13-21. How does it make you feel to know that Jesus was thinking of you before His time on the cross?

2. Who do you lock arms with to get through your seasons of loneliness?

3. Do you know someone walking through a deep place? Write out your prayer for him or her. Look for a time this week you can spend some time together.

4. Other than the face to face, what do you look forward to about heaven? What do you think it will be like? What is the first thing you want to do when you get there? What do you think it means to live life with eternal perspective?

Further Text
Read John 14:1-3.

Chapter 7
One Perfect Gift

Soundtrack
"Grace," by Laura Story
"All Who Are Thirsty," by Kutless

Questions
1. What is the sweetest gift you've ever received? Who was it from? Why is it still so special to you? If you're doing this study with a small group (and the gift is portable), bring it along so you can show it off. You may also want to think of the most bizarre, the funniest, or the most memorable gift you've ever received.

2. How is God's love like a gift to you? How does it show in your life? Do you think you're "living the gift"? If not, what's holding you back?

3. Even though Jesus returned to heaven, He left the Holy Spirit to dwell inside us. Paul tells us there are specific ways the Holy Spirit manifests in our lives. In Galatians 5, he calls them the "fruit of the Spirit." Take a look at Galatians 5:16-22. Which "fruit" do you see evidenced most in your life? Which one isn't?

Further Text
Read Luke 2.

Chapter 8
Pianos and Paintbrushes

Soundtrack
"Adoration," by Matthew Glass
"Here I Am to Worship," by Tim Hughes

Questions
1. When you hear the word "worship," what is the first image that comes to mind?

2. Think of the most memorable time you've spent in worship. What about that experience made it worship full of "spirit and truth"?

3. Take the time to read Paul's full sermon to the people of Athens in Acts 17:16-34. As is typical of his style, Paul was well acquainted with Greek culture—everything from its art (he mentions the Greek poets in this passage) to its misplaced worship. Do you think Athens was anything like your culture? What part of Paul's message resonates most strongly to you?

Further Reflection

Consider worshiping God in a new way this week. Psalm 96:1 tells us to sing a "new song" unto the Lord (see also Ps. 40:3; 98:1). For me, the most liberating thing about a "new song" moment is that I don't know the motions. I don't have the words memorized and I may feel a bit awkward and out of my comfort zone. Maybe you could attend a church service with a different style of music. Or maybe you could try worship alone instead of with a group of people. Or maybe you could drive up to a mountain somewhere—get out in the nature that David wrote about so much—and worship God from the highest hills. After you do this, write out your experience. Don't forget it. Sporadic moments of worship can be some of the sweetest and most intimate moments with God you'll experience in this lifetime.

Further Text

Another excellent story about worship is the story of Shadrach, Meshach and Abednego in Daniel 3. All three young men stood alone in a culture consumed with idol worship and refused to bend their knees to anyone but the true God. Take some time to read their story, and then write your favorite verse (or verses) in the margin. Is their culture anything like yours? What else did you learn about worship when you read this passage?

Chapter 9
Love that Moves

Soundtrack

"What Are You Waiting For?" by Natalie Grant
"Mighty to Save," by Hillsong United

Questions

1. Ask God to bring to mind one person you can serve this week. It may be someone in your school, on your campus,

or in your office. Then spend some time each day praying for that person. What's a random (or maybe even unknown) act of kindness you can do for him or her? If this person isn't your friend already, could you make an effort to pull him or her into your circle?

2. The disciples are MIA through most of the conversation at the well. Although they may have arrived just in time to hear Jesus declare Himself to be the Messiah, they missed most of this important conversation. As Sam runs back to the village, they encourage Jesus to eat, and He tells them He has "food" they don't understand. Do you think sometimes you miss out on seeing God do something amazing because your focus is off? Is it possible to miss out on knowing God even when you're involved in ministry? How do you decide which people and activities get priority in your life?

3. What are some of the most prominent needs in your community? (Do the research—rightnow.org is a good place to start.) Do any of those needs resonate in your heart? Your time is a precious gift. If you had one hour each week to share God's love through your time, energy and talents, what would you do with that hour?

4. What about the world at large? Check out the list on pages 182-184. Are there any of those issues you want to pursue? Is there a way you could grab a group of girls and go serve one weekend?

Further Reflection

Take some time to read about a woman who carried God's love into the world. Grab your library card and see if you can find *Ruth: A Portrait*, Patricia Cornwall's autobiography of Ruth Bell Graham, or *A Chance to Die*, Elisabeth Elliot's book on the life of Amy Carmichael.

Further Text
Read Matthew 28:16 and Philippians 1:20-22.

Chapter 10
Paper Violets

Soundtrack
"Legacy," by Nichole Nordeman
"Captivated," by Vicky Beeching

Questions

1. Imagine the Samaritan woman 20 years after the scene by the well takes place. If a visitor came through Sychar and stopped by Jacob's Well, what do you think the Samaritan woman would talk about? How do you think she would describe her conversation with Jesus?

2. Think of someone you know who is making (or has made) a profound impact on your life. What about that person's legacy resonates most with you?

3. If you're doing this study with a small group, take some time to affirm the strengths you see in each other. Take a look back at the fruit of the Spirit in Galatians 5:16-22 and identify which trait is strongest in each person. What legacy are the girls in your group leaving?

4. Now that we've come to the end of the story, reread John 4:4-42 one more time. What was your favorite verse in this scene by the well? What verse resonates most strongly in your life at this point? If you've read this story before, how was it different to you this time?

Further Reflection
Consider buying a cheap journal. On the first page, write your favorite verse from the story by the well (or any other passage of

Scripture that you discovered while doing this study). On the second page, write the date, and—at this exact moment—what you want your legacy to be. How do you see God working in this season of your life? How are you sharing his love with the world? What message will you carry? What "Samaria" do you want the courage to run back into? What frustrates you the most about your journey with God right now? Take some time to personalize the journal and then save it. Consider going back to it yearly and writing a new entry. Think about how your legacy is refining and molding into something that lasts far beyond your lifetime.

Further Text
Read Philippians 1:21 and 4:4-9.

Ready to Move?

If you need a jump start on figuring out ways to use your talent, passion, time, and energy to serve other people, take a look at the following sites:

Right Now
www.rightnow.org

Compassion International
www.compassion.com

Operation Smile
operationsmile.org

Blood Water Mission
www.bloodwatermission.com

Habitat for Humanity
www.habitat.org

Brio Missions
www.briomag.com/missions

YWAM
www.ywam.org

The Junky Car Club
www.junkycarclub.com

Rosa Loves
www.rosaloves.com

Samaritan's Purse
www.samaritanspurse.org

The Home Foundation
www.thehomefoundation.net

Surviving the Deep

You do not, and should not, face the deep alone. Not only is God close to you through seasons of pain, but He also gives you a community of fellow believers who will walk beside you. If you're experiencing any kind of deep pain, don't untangle the grief alone. Find someone to talk to immediately, whether it's your parents, your pastor, your student director, a coach or a mentor. Certified Christian counselors (who your pastor can probably help you locate) are trained to help regular folks like me and you overcome addictions and obsessions. A trained counselor can also walk with you through the stages of grief, provide a listening ear, and help you slowly move back into the world (see www.aacc.net). Other resources for deep places:

Mercy Ministries
www.mercyministries.org

To Write Love on Her Arms
www.twloha.com

Acknowledgments

I'm sitting here on my front porch at my favorite time of day: that last little slip of time between day and night, trying to figure out the right way to say thank you to some people. It took awhile for this book to flair out of my heart and onto paper. Were it not for the passion, scholarship and talent of so many individuals, it would never be in your hands. I am so grateful for what they brought to this journey and what they bring to my life. I wish I could personally introduce them to you. And I wish I was a good enough writer to describe what they mean to me. Here goes my best effort:

My mom was my first reader, but, more importantly, she was my dearest friend and encourager throughout the writing of this book. She's the kind of woman who doesn't just march to her own drumbeat but dances to it as well, and I love having her in my life. My dad, the most kind and most hilarious man I know, frequently took me out for dinner and coffee breaks during my writing haze. He's my biggest cheerleader, without a doubt. When I was a little girl, my dad told me a face without freckles was like a sky without stars, and I've never forgotten it. Every girl deserves parents who tell her she's beautiful, especially when she can't see it herself. It makes navigating these paperdoll years much easier. "Thank you" hardly does them justice.

My gorgeous older sister, Bridgett, and her sweet family put up with me for weeks at a time while I was working. When I finally left, they called just to remind me they loved me. My brother, Chase, drove me up to the mountains for coffee and Coldplay when I needed to clear my head. They keep me rooted in the kind of love that matters and lasts. It is impossible to be paper around them. I love them more than they can possibly understand.

I'm thankful for my fabulous editor, Kim Bangs, who believed in this message and encouraged me from start to finish. I'm also grateful to the creative team at Regal who took every piece of this project, from the cover to the copywriting, and made it more beautiful than I imagined.

Several families and individuals made it possible for me to pursue some grad work, and I know this book (and my life) was enhanced by that experience. Even though I know they would want to remain anonymous, their act of kindness has blessed my life in more ways than I can ever articulate.

Susie Shellenberger has been a mentor and friend to me for many years now. I'm grateful for her friendship and encouragement. I love my *Brio* family to pieces. It was an honor to be a tiny part of what they do each month.

I am grateful for my friend Shannon Ethridge, who wrote a beautiful foreword for this book. Her encouragement to start and finish this project, and to keep overcoming all these insecurities and fears in my own journey, has been paramount.

I'm grateful to Greg Johnson for finding a perfect home for my *Paperdoll*.

Gene and Harriet Bond gave me my first job as a youth intern out of college. What I thought would last a short summer became three years that healed my heart in ways I never thought possible. One of the best parts was sitting at their table once a week, eating cookies, and spending time with them. They loved me, and believed in me, through all the hard places. For the ways they poured into my life, I cannot thank them enough.

I'm grateful to the students at NHBC for three years of Uno tournaments, camel rides, bus trips, Bible study, water balloons, karaoke, burnt cookies and pink flamingoes. I don't think I ever ministered to you half the way you ministered to me. You will change the world, no doubt about it. Consider me your permanent standing ovation.

Thank you again to the Hughett and Carroll family, especially to Terri and Katie, for allowing me to share your story.

I am grateful to friends who read this manuscript and made it better, particularly to Kaylene Whitaker and Jill Zwyghuizen, who looked at parts of this story as friends, scholars and fellow day trippers to the well. They also taught me how to merge in Dallas traffic, which is quite an accomplishment in itself.

During the writing of this book, many couples and families opened their homes to me. Sometimes I just stayed for a weekend and sometimes (for the, um, lucky ones) I stayed a whole summer. Thanks to the Zdanios, the Asburys, the Brickmans, the Slaytons, the Evelands and Aunt Lillie for giving me a home away from home and making me feel like family.

I am grateful to the Panera and Starbucks chains in Chattanooga for not kicking me out even when I stayed for hours but only bought tea.

Thanks to you, whoever you are, for walking to the well with me. It's good to know that we aren't on this journey alone, isn't it?

And last (because this is my favorite thank you) I am grateful to the One who thought I was worth waiting for. I hope these jumbled up words bring You glory. I can't wait for the face to face. You are, truly, my freefall.

Love,
Natalie

More Great Resources from
Regal Books

Beautiful
How to Be a Woman of God
Beth Redman
ISBN 978.08307.41984
ISBN 08307.41984

Eyes Wide Open
Avoiding the Heartbreak of Emotional Promiscuity
Brienne Murk
ISBN 978.08307.44923
ISBN 08307.44924

The Naked Truth
About Sex, Love and Relationships
Lakita Garth
ISBN 978.08307.43285
ISBN 08307.43286

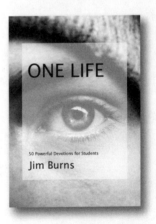

One Life
50 Powerful Devotions for Students
Jim Burns
ISBN 978.08307.43049
ISBN 08307.43049